DEVELOPING LITERATURE-BASED READING PROGRAMS

A How-To-Do-It Manual

BERNICE L. YESNER
M. MARY MURRAY

*HOW-TO-DO-IT MANUALS FOR
SCHOOL AND PUBLIC LIBRARIANS*

*Number 13
Series Editor: Barbara L. Stein*

NEAL-SCHUMAN PUBLISHERS, INC.
New York, London

Published by Neal-Schuman Publishers, Inc.
100 Varick Street
New York, NY 10013

Copyright © 1993 by Bernice L. Yesner and M. Mary Murray

Printed and bound in the United States of America

Library of Congress Cataloging-in-Publication Data

Yesner, Bernice L.
    Developing literature-based reading programs : a how-to-do-it
manual for librarians / Bernice L. Yesner, M. Mary Murray.
        p.   cm. — (How-to-do-it manuals for school and public
librarians ; no. 13)
    Includes bibliographical references and index.
    ISBN 1-55570-122-1
    1. School libraries—Activity programs—United States.   2. Reading
(Elementary—United States.   3. Literature—Study and teaching
(Elementary—United States.   I. Murray, M. (mary), 1925-   .
II. Title.   III. Series.
Z675.S3Y46   1993
027.8'222'0973—dc20   93-5493
                                                                                         CIP

CONTENTS

PREFACE

Developing Literature-Based Reading Programs was written to help classroom teachers, reading specialists, library media professionals, curriculum directors, principals, and district administrators formulate and implement plans for effective literature-based reading programs. Such concepts as *whole language, literature-based basals*, or *graded literature reading programs* are not always defined clearly. *Developing Literature-Based Reading Programs* explains the similarities and differences of these approaches to teaching reading. Realistic methods that have proven valid in promoting, planning, installing, and running a literature-based reading program are set forth in detail.

Chapter 1 describes both the basal reading and whole language movements, and outlines the differences between the two. We then describe the literature-based reading program and give practical applications for its use. In the second chapter, we discuss current research in teaching skills and phonics, and how it applies to the literature-based reading program.

In the next three chapters, we get down to the details. Chapter 3 gives the background: planning, organizing, and starting literature-based reading programs. The organization of the program is detailed in chapter 4, and in chapter 5 we look at the acquisition and processing of the materials needed for the program's collection.

Parents are always important in any learning process, and in chapter 6 we examine their role in this type of program. Any lingering questions that may be left after this discussion are covered in chapter 7. Finally, we end with a list of titles recommended for a literature-based reading programs.

Of paramount importance in launching a successful program is close cooperation between reading teachers, classroom teachers, and library media specialists. The library media specialist, a certified teacher as well as an expert on learning materials, can and should be a leader in the move toward a literature-based reading program.

Library media collections in schools contemplating such a program probably already contain most, if not all, of the titles that will be considered for the final list. In times of fiscal restraint and curtailed budgets, the permanent housing of literature-based reading materials in each classroom is neither a wise use of funds nor is it best for the teaching/learning process. A collection that circulates from the library media center allows teachers to use the materials when they need them—giving most effective support to the curriculum.

Teachers and students who are involved in literature-based reading programs are the best advocates for such programs. Teachers attest to the excitement of teaching this way; whether by theme approach or integrated curriculum. The students enjoy the wide variety of topics, themes, characters, and settings. Most of all, they enjoy reading so many wonderful books.

To paraphrase an old commercial, "Try it, you'll like it!"

Bernice L. Yesner
M. Mary Murray

1 LITERATURE-BASED READING: WHOLE LANGUAGE CONTEXT

Before plunging into a literature-based reading program, it will be important to define clearly what it is and how it works. This is essential for those who will implement it and for those who will give it the go-ahead: upper level administrators including superintendents, curriculum directors, or supervisors, and principals. Their role will be to explain to the Board of Education and to parents what literature-based reading is and why it is desirable. This chapter and the next will provide you with theoretical arguments for supporting such a program, as well as guidance for classroom teachers and reading specialists who wish to start a literature-based program on a small scale in their classrooms and reading labs. The purpose here is to give information and help convince decision makers that the movement into literature-based reading is worthwhile.

A SHORT HISTORY OF THE BASAL READING MOVEMENT

Before the 1880s, reading instruction in the United States had the development of patriotism as a primary focus. "Readers" used in schools were also heavily laced with religious references. In the early part of the 1880s, this practice gave way to a concern for cultural development. Reading instruction was now seen as a medium for ". . .awakening a permanent interest in literary material which would be a cultural asset to the individual in adult life" (Smith 1986, 115). The previous focus on drill and practice was replaced by a new emphasis on giving children a "taste for good literature" (Smith 1986, 116). For a short while, reading educators used quality literature as the basis for instruction.

The advent of the testing movement in the United States profoundly affected reading instruction in ways that are still felt. The introduction of a handwriting scale by Thorndike in 1909 initiated the movement toward also breaking reading down into manageable, testable units. As a result of this new emphasis and the proliferation of tests in all areas of the curriculum, reading educators were forced to design tests of comprehension based on silent reading, thus deemphasizing the more prevalent mode of oral reading instruction. At that point, reading books containing short stories with controlled vocabularies written at graded levels of difficulty were developed by publishers to foster silent reading comprehension (Smith 1986, 163). Teachers, of course, rising to the challenge, began to create exercises that would foster growth in silent reading comprehension. The publishers, not to be outdone, created workbooks with exercises to help children practice those skills that would make them better comprehenders. Along with the readers and workbooks were tests which helped teachers determine a child's level of performance in these skills. Thus, we saw the birth of the basal reading system in the United States.

From the 1920s to the present, the basal reading system has prevailed as the most popular method of teaching reading in public and in many private schools. It has become one of the most sophisticated educational tools used in schools. Not only are materials constructed for use at designated grade levels, but teachers' manuals provide everything needed to run a reading program in the classroom. Indeed, they are so well developed that teachers are given step-by-step instructions in the presentation of a reading lesson. How to begin, how to ask questions, and how to teach skills are well spelled out as are ideas for reinforcing skills after workbook pages are completed. In essence, teachers could easily put aside all the strategies they learned in college for fostering reading development. The teachers' manual provides everything needed to teach reading in a tried and true format that is exceptionally well organized. When using it, a teacher doesn't have to think very much, and in fact, neither do the students.

ENTER THE WHOLE LANGUAGE MOVEMENT

> . . . language development is
> incremental, learned, and
> culturally based.
>
> **Holdaway**

In the 1970s a book came out of New Zealand that became a bible of sorts for a new movement in language arts instruction. Written by Don Holdaway, who lived and taught in New Zealand, *The Foundations of Literacy* (Holdaway 1979) chronicled his personal experiences as a reading teacher and the journey he took into the world of the young child learning to read. Holdaway did not devise a new method of teaching reading. Rather, he studied how children advanced into literacy and he suggested that literacy development is a matter of language development. It has many human dimensions, it is incremental, it is learned, and it is a cultural matter. He further suggested that reading acquisition, like spoken language acquisition, is a developmental process which has the following characteristics:

1. Immersion: The child learns any skill best by being immersed in an environment in which the skill is constantly being used.

2. Emulation: The child must be exposed to lively examples of the skill being learned from the adults in his or her daily life. What is seen and heard must be true to life, of the best quality, and have utilitarian value for the child.

3. Reinforcement: The child needs opportunities to practice the skill being learned and rewards for the effort.

4. Approximations: The child is allowed and encouraged to try the skill and to come as close as possible to the "real thing" without fear of being "wrong."

5. Practice: The child is encouraged to practice the skill but is allowed to do so at a pace that is comfortable.

6. Secure Environment: The learning environment is a place free of threat where help is readily available for the learner.

7. Development Proceeds Differently: Not every child will develop at the same pace. It is possible for two or more children of the same age to be at entirely different stages of development.

From these principles of developmental learning emerged the concept of whole language learning. Holdaway and other whole language theorists hoped to get teachers and other educators to think about how a child learns and to apply those principles to literacy instruction. If an educator does embrace the concept, it will change the way that the teacher introduces children to the reading process.

If the idea that language learning, whether oral or written, is best learned in an environment where language is being used in useful ways to achieve authentic ends, then the child will need to see and hear the very best in written and spoken discourse. This means that both the home and school must have examples of good literature for the children to see and hear. The text should have natural language with which the child can identify, a certain rhythmic appeal, it must have a predictable quality so that the child can anticipate what is coming in the text, and an accessible sense of sequence which will assist the child's comprehension.

In a whole language environment, then, one will find whole texts, both big books for whole-group experiences and small books for individual exploration. Also available will be charts with poems and rhymes having a kind of musical appeal for the children. Both books and charts will be used for instruction in phonics, word analysis, and language study.

Children will not only see and hear good language, they will be encouraged to create language in both written and spoken format, and explore the possibilities of writing from the time they enter school at an early age. As they move through the grades, they will write their own poems and plays as well as do research using nonfiction materials. In every way they will explore language and grow in its use in an environment that encourages experimentation without fear of failing to meet expectations.

It was from these principles that the literature-based movement evolved. While it is possible to use literature texts in an essentially traditional model of reading instruction, the impetus for breaking away from such use came from the whole language movement.

HOW TO RECOGNIZE A LITERATURE-BASED CLASSROOM

There should be more going on in a literature-based classroom than simply using entire real books in place of basal reading materials. In his description of a model of literature learning, Brian Cambourne, an Australian educator and researcher of literacy development, suggests that the following *Conditions of Learning* (Cambourne, 1989) will be present in a classroom where growth in literacy is fostered:

1. Immersion: The students will be immersed in a wide range of texts exhibiting rich language. Therefore the literacy classroom will have books and charts and posters of every conceivable size and shape not only visible but well within the reach of the children.

2. Demonstration: The children will see how expert readers and writers engage themselves with print. They will see the teacher read silently and out loud to them, write while they write, and demonstrate strategies that they can use to deal with a challenging text.

3. Engagement: Students will be encouraged to try to read and write knowing that the teacher expects them to succeed and will support their efforts even if they fail the first few times.

4. Responsibility: Students in this environment have a clear understanding that the responsibility for their learning is as much theirs as it is the teacher's. At no time will the teacher usurp control over their learning.

5. Employment: There will be time and opportunity for the child to practice the skills being learned, in this case reading, writing, listening, and speaking.

6. Approximation: Adapted from Holdaway's concept, the child soon learns that learning is not being correct, but is rather the opportunity to approximate the skill until mastery is achieved. In other words, the children keep trying until they get it right.

How do we transfer all of this into a traditional classroom model using a basal system? Holdaway tells us that it comes down to seeing a difference between skill instruction and instruction in the use of strategies. In skill instruction, the teacher essentially instructs the students how to perform the skill and then corrects them if they perform it incorrectly. In strategy instruction, the teacher guides the student in the use of a specific strategy and then invites him or her to self-correct the response. The teacher steps back and supports the student's attempt to take control of the learning while remaining available for support if needed.

The major difference in Holdaway's view is the "presence or absence of self-direction on the part of the learner" (Holdaway 1979, 136). This is a crucial point regarding whole language philosophy. It is often assumed that drawing a distinction between "skills" instruction and "strategies" instruction implies that whole language theorists are suggesting that it is unnecessary or undesirable to teach skills. Just the opposite is true: they are saying that *how* skills are taught has to be rethought and redesigned. They are suggesting that teaching skills in isolation is undesirable. There are, however, some whole language advocates who express the view that the teacher should address the skill only when the child is ready to deal with it. This will in all likelihood continue to be one of the most hotly debated points related to the whole language movement.

What, then, will we find going on in a literature-based/whole language literacy classroom? Newman (1985) describes it this way:

1. Only complete forms of written language such as stories, novels, signs and such things as cereal boxes will be used for instruction or pleasure reading.
2. Children in this classroom will be invited to experiment with language and expectations for "correctness" will not be present.
3. Rather than being corrected, children will be encouraged to judge for themselves whether or not what they are reading makes sense.

4. Predictable books which have repetitive language patterns which help the child anticipate what is coming next will be widely used. Such pieces of literature as songs, nursery rhymes, poems, and contemporary as well as classical literature will be in place.
5. Both oral and written language experience stories will be used with the children on a regular basis.
6. Shared reading using big books will be done regularly.
7. Story reading will occur frequently. At times, adults or older students will read to the younger children and at other times the younger children will take the stage and read to an older person.
8. Sustained silent reading (SSR) will occur ideally on a daily basis. SSR allows an opportunity for students at all grade levels to spend some period of time during the school day reading for pleasure. It is a time set aside in the schedule during which all instruction stops while both teacher and students take out their books and read.
9. Children's trade books will be used for instruction in place of basal materials.

This is probably a good time to address the one issue that will receive the most attention in the decision to change from the use of basals to the use of literature books and materials as a means of reading instruction, namely, why are trade books more desirable instructional tools than basal reading materials?

WHY USE TRADE BOOKS RATHER THAN BASAL MATERIALS?

In order to answer this question, we must consider the purpose or goal of reading instruction. Volumes have already been written on this topic and volumes more could and probably will be written on it. For our purposes we will reflect upon the thoughts of those reading educators who have gained some prominence due to their efforts and expertise in reading instruction.

In his treatise on literacy learning, Holdaway, arguing against the premise that print will soon become an outdated medium, suggests that if we accept the theory that language is a "coded transaction of meanings rather than an inventory of vocabulary strung together according to grammatical rules" then we must rethink our methods of instruction (Holdaway 1984, 6). He refers to the newer research in reading that establishes the reader as an active participant in the reading process. No longer do we see meaning as residing wholly in the text waiting to be unlocked by the reader who would use certain word attack skills and context clues. We now view the meaning one gets from text as being unlocked by a combination of the reader's background knowledge and the use of certain strategies which include but are not limited to word attack and vocabulary skills. The reader's life experience, motivations, self esteem, and expectations also count.

Marilyn Jaeger Adams tells us that the task of reading educators of the future will be to prepare children with the ability to "acquire, understand, use, and communicate information accurately, efficiently and independently" (Adams 1990, 26). Marie Clay says that reading involves "messages expressed in language. . . knowing about direction rules of printed language, space formats, and punctuation cues. . .(and) visual patterns" (Clay 1979, 7). Further definitions of reading include those offered by the writers of the national report on reading entitled *Becoming a Nation of Readers*. They describe reading simply as "the process of constructing meaning from written texts" (Anderson, et al. 1984, 7).

Reading is getting meaning from printed material using our own background knowledge and recommended strategies to interact with the text and to thereby create meaning. It is not a static process but rather very dynamic and ongoing. It relies upon many factors for success in ultimately comprehending the message conveyed by the author. Namely, we will comprehend to the extent that our knowledge about the topic is current and relevant, and to the extent that the strategies we use to deal with print are well enough established to allow us to try to figure out unknown words or nebulous literary or content-specific terms. Those components of print knowledge that Clay refers to would need to be well established for all of this to work, of course.

There is also one component of the process that affects our comprehension of written matter which is often overlooked but is nonetheless integral to good comprehension: the text itself. The impact of the quality of writing on the comprehension of the author's message rests at the heart of the issue of using good literature in reading instruction.

Let us consider this point in more detail by looking at this passage from the classic fairy tale "The Shoemaker and the Elves":

> As soon as it was midnight they saw come in two neatly formed naked little men, who seated themselves before the shoemaker's table, and took up the work that was already prepared, and began to stitch, to pierce, and to hammer so cleverly and so quickly with their fingers that the shoemaker's eyes could scarcely follow them, so full of wonder was he (Johnson, Sickels & Sayers 1970, 124).

The charm of this scene painted with words was altered by a basal reader publisher in an adaptation of this story written for a primary-level child. This is their version:

> Tap, tap, tap. See me work. I make good things. See the red ones. See the yellow ones. No, no, no. I do not want red ones. I do not want yellow ones. I want green ones.

Comparing one version with the other, it is easy to see that the second one was designed to be used for instruction with children who are in the early stages of reading development. The sentences are short, the words are simple and could easily be read by a child with average reading ability in the first grade. At no point is the word elves used and the object being worked upon is not named. Imagine a child reading this without the benefit of a picture to give clues. It is clear that comprehension of this story is not of prime importance. Rather, the publisher probably had in mind using the words to reinforce some phonetic skill or to introduce new vocabulary.

The purpose of basal reader stories is essentially, to use text to teach skills. As a result, the language that authors come up with is often stilted and unnatural. Remember what was said earlier about the importance of having natural language in the child's environment to foster literacy development. Children do not hear short choppy sentences being spoken at home or, it is to be hoped, in the classroom. Why then would a publisher employ such language in the instructional materials used to teach reading? Is it because there is a fear that if vocabulary is not controlled then children will not learn to read?

In 1987, the National Council of Teachers of English held a two-day conference on the basal reader. The results of that meeting were presented the following spring at the International Reading Association annual convention in Toronto, Canada. The report, entitled *Report Card on Basal Readers*, commented on the use of controlled vocabulary to produce stories for basal readers and is summarized for us in this statement about the report:

> *Report Card* reminds us that such text is not natural language, and it is therefore unpredictable for the learner; it would never occur outside of a pre-primer. The purpose is obviously to teach words. The pre-primer stories are proof that there is more concern for presenting and controlling vocabulary than for telling an interesting or predictable and thus easy-to-read story (Watson & Weaver 1988, 2).

Holdaway refers to such stories as an example of "semilanguage which has been denatured in the interests of controlling vocabulary or phonic regularity" (Holdaway 1984, 6). The Shoemaker story is one example of a publisher's attempt to simplify a passage in the interests of skill development while ignoring the comprehension of the text. As a result of these types of intervention, stories that have inherent appeal and a certain simplicity are stripped not only of their ability to engage the child's interest but also their ability to be comprehended. Shorter sentences with simple words do not always add up to easy-to-read text.

In addition to the previously mentioned points related to basal reader stories, the following reasons for using literature in the reading program are offered:

1. *Literature allows meaning to dominate.* The importance of connecting reading to thinking is suggested here.
2. *Literature use concentrates on the development of readers rather than the development of skills.* This speaks for itself.

3. *Literature promotes positive self-concepts in beginning readers*. Routman tells us that children in a literature-based environment tend to think of themselves as readers regardless of their ability and background.
4. *Literature promotes language development*. The presence of complex language patterns and figurative language in good literature aids comprehension and vocabulary development according to Routman.
5. *Literature promotes fluent reading*. Through oral reading of stories having predictable patterns and sequences, children come to read with understanding as opposed to word-by-word reading.
6. *Literature deals with human emotions*. Greater interest in reading is generated when real-life stories are used. Students come to identify with characters.
7. *Literature exposes students to a variety of story structures, themes, and authors' styles*. This ultimately has a direct impact upon student's writing practices.
8. *Literature puts children in contact with illustration at its best*. This often creates greater interest in stories.
9. *Literature makes reading fun*. If we wish to make lifelong readers of our students, we must accept the importance of this point (Routman 1988, 20-22).

Cullinan tells us that literature feeds the fancy. . .informs the imagination and feeds the desire to read (Cullinan 1987, 6). If it is our goal to make good readers out of our students we cannot ignore the fact that they must do a lot of reading, not only in school but also on their own at home. Educators who have worked with children for any length of time realize that making learning seem as though it is fun is half the battle of getting students to learn. So if we wish to have them read, we must create in them a love of reading. It is the contention of literature-based reading proponents that the use of literature in the reading program will do just that. The bottom line is that enjoyment of reading leads to more reading which leads to sustained—often life long— literacy.

It must be remembered that literature is not confined to fictional stories. Recent years have seen publication of a greatly increased number of easily read nonfiction books which offer young readers discovery of themselves and the world around them and recognition, confirmation perhaps, of their own wonderings and conjectures.

PRACTICAL APPLICATIONS

The poets warned us that all that glitters is not gold and we must acknowledge that all programs called "whole language" are not necessarily what they claim to be. The market is flooded with packaged deals from publishers, jobbers, prebinders, school supply houses, and various promoters eager to cash in on a new buzzword. The term, which is either completely misunderstood or deliberately misconstrued for profit's sake, is scarcely better perceived by educators including those who profess to practice the whole language approach. Library media specialists need to understand it, be able to explain it compellingly, and advocate it.

The whole language perspective is neither a philosophy nor a method. It deals with how children learn, with what language is, and with how language learning takes place. It embodies all the linguistic and sociolinguistic systems and subsystems. It is called "whole" language because the emphasis is on the entirety of language. Thus, in the classroom the teacher creates situations and contexts wherein the children learn the wholeness of language. The setting of the classroom abounds with examples of written language, especially those of which the students are the authors, as well as quotations and short poems. In the classrooms of pre-readers and blossoming readers there are works created by individual students, small groups, or the class as a whole, which have been transcribed by the teacher so that all may see what the students composed. Children are assisted in becoming writers before they can write on their own. Authorship or ownership of their language is of paramount importance.

Adults read aloud a great deal from a wide variety of good children's literature throughout the grade levels. While exposure to enriched language has merits all its own, the material read aloud is not confined to poetry or fiction. It may include biography, history as presented in journals, an essay, or an onlooker's report of a sporting event. Thus learners are exposed to all kinds of language and a variety of styles of expression of both language meant to be written and oral language that has been put into written form.

M.A.K. Halliday acknowledges the differences in learning styles of children, some relying more on sight, others on hearing. He also points out that variations in teaching styles depend on the teacher's comfort in using one or another. But he emphasizes that "reading/writing and listening/speaking are different ways of learning because they are different ways of knowing." He sees written language as a synoptic view of the world, a product rather than a process. The spoken language, on the other hand, he sees as a dynamic view of the world.

Further, Halliday states that there are inherently different properties in written and spoken language whether the written language is read aloud or the spoken language is transcribed into printed text. He deplores the overemphasis on written language at the risk of undervaluing spoken language. We who educate children need to heed his caveats and to make sure that all forms of spoken and written language are part of their learning experiences.

Brian Cambourne states that "learning to become literate ought to be as uncomplicated and barrier-free as possible." By literate he means not only being able to read well but also to write, spell, and punctuate properly. He differentiates between struggling and suffering. The former is an essential part of learning and brings with it a kind of exultation when the problem is solved or the difficulty mastered. When the struggle goes to the extent of suffering and tedium breeds boredom, learning is scant, ineffective, or nonexistent. Cambourne also believes that "once learned, the skills of literacy should be durable." When children experience the success of reading for information, escape, pleasure, etc., they must continue this enjoyment beyond schooling to become lifelong readers. They must also become lifelong writers to underscore learning, help delineate and solve problems, and communicate with friends or colleagues.

SETTING A GOOD EXAMPLE

In addition to the nonfragmented approach being demonstrated by teachers there also needs to be modeling by them as well. *Teachers must be seen as readers, writers, and learners themselves.* They must also exhibit correct use of language, and respect and enthusiasm for language, regardless of the grade level or subject areas in which they specialize. Administrators should hold this as a priority when considering applicants for teaching positions and be vigilant in their observations of faculty in the classroom and throughout the school complex. Ungrammatical and/or misspelled notes to parents will undo the benefits of countless science fairs, concerts, or gymkhanas. If we are to maintain a high standard for the students it must apply to educators as well.

It is interesting that in the great debate about the teaching/learning of reading, there seems to be no dissent amongst the hundreds of gurus about the importance of reading aloud to children from infancy onward. There are no warnings about the necessity for reading only those materials that are at the child's age level, grade level, or reading ability level determined by whatever formula is currently in vogue. The important thing is the reading. Further, there is proven value in having children see adults, especially in their homes, reading books, magazines, and newspapers as part of their daily lives. There is overwhelming evidence of the benefits that result.

INTEGRATING SKILLS

There has been criticism of the whole language approach among phonics advocates, on the grounds it provides no phonics instruction. There may be some teachers who profess to use whole language who are not giving phonics instruction to their students, but the fault is in their application, not in the concept. The unfragmented approach does not mean there is no attention to the form or structure of language; quite the contrary. These same critics declare that minority or immigrant students or those who come from homes where reading is undervalued need more practice and drill. But we are talking about students becoming literate, not merely decoders. We want more than children who *can* read. We want children who *do* read, because they *can* and *want* to.

It is not uncommon to hear children read from their basals without hesitation or mistake and still be unable to explain what they have just read. Decoding has little to do with comprehension. If students do not understand what they read in the primary grades they may fall farther and farther behind as the subject matter increases in complexity. It is the wholeness of the language that enables beginning readers to comprehend and enjoy the clues to understanding that lead to true learning.

Whole Language proponents point out that minority and immigrant children, or those from different cultures, benefit from the climate of the whole language classroom in which the curriculum and activities are adapted to the children. A large component is the respect for children as they are, as well as for their interests and their needs. This is one reason why a library media program is essential in the school and that the library media teachers are copractitioners of the whole language effort. As resource specialists, storytellers, and experts in the world of children's and young adults' literature they are more than mere allies of the classroom teachers. They must be able to recommend materials, additional titles to those currently in use, possible themes or topics, and interdisciplinary approaches.

Adopting the literature-based aspect of the whole language approach in the classroom is more work than the traditional systems and it is a lot more exciting, stimulating, and rewarding for the teacher. The basal-dependent teacher could use texts and tests (supplied by the same publishers) year after year. In whole language the class as well as the teacher will have options as to the topics chosen, the materials used, methodology, and assessment. Whole language flourishes in schools where textbooks are no longer used and literature-based, resource-based learning is the armature of the curriculum.

But getting rid of the basals will not guarantee that teachers will not "basalize" the literature the children read. This bastardization of the whole language movement by basal publishers and other promoters is understandable as well as regrettable. They are not about to let their tightly controlled empire slip away. Since teachers are loaded with work, and are human beings, they are perfect targets for the "tell you what I'm going to do" approach of the commercial pitch. There are packages (available for large sums of money, of course) that will provide phonics lessons, activities, and end-of-chapter tests, etc. Teachers are not the only targets of these phony "whole language programs" as ads in professional journals for administrators will attest. Administrators are enticed to buy the packages so that whole language can be instantly brought into every classroom. Some advocates of literature-based reading programs point out that, at least, the children would be reading whole books and not the snippets of the basal. But if the teachers are tearing the literature apart to make sure the phonics instruction, drill, and end-of-chapter tests are all plentiful, they have destroyed the literature and ruined the name of whole literature while never properly practicing it. What is worse, they may have spoiled the children's enjoyment of good writing and good authors.

For a period of time there was a tendency on the part of educators of preschool children to avoid the teaching of reading and writing. There was also the effort to discourage the interference of parents in the effort. In some cases it was taken to the extreme of not even allowing the children to see printed material. Patrick Shannon believes it might have been an attempt to protect the children from adult pressures. Perhaps it was the reaction to the rigid methods that had previously been used with nursery school children. The developmentally appropriate education of young children which is prevalent today faces the behavior of the children as they are. This means that many are already scribbling in simulation of adult writing, they understand what printed language is, and they may recognize many letters.

The kindergarten is often an extended day or full day for many children, and it is at this level where we see remarkable variances in children's facility with language in oral forms as well as in reading and writing. The exposure to books with simple sentences (such as the Big Books offer) may lead to memorization of the text. This is partly through the repetition within the text itself and partly through repeated exposure to favorite stories which the children favor. Classroom discussions and teacher-directed activities will provide variations on a theme to reinforce what has been learned as well as to extend the learning. Chants, which are repetitious in form, when printed out and read with the children are variants that lead to beginning, independent reading skills.

The concommitant writing development will include the creative spelling which may begin with a single letter used for a word. The next stage is one which may see more consonants with few or no vowels. Parents and other relatives are sometimes horrified to find that the teachers do not correct this writing and worry that bad habits are being allowed to form which may be difficult to break. Often these fears are based on their own difficulties with spelling. It is important that teachers take time to explain process writing as well as child development. Children, by nature, want to turn out good product and they will understand the need for drafting, editing, and rewriting—all in good time.

WORKING TOGETHER

Parents have many vital roles to play in the emerging literacy of their children. We have already mentioned the importance of reading aloud to children from early infancy. Parents need to show the value of reading by modeling the behavior: reading aloud signs as they drive or walk with the children; having available and using newspapers, magazines, and books; creating opportunities for children to attempt or pretend reading and writing (for fun, not lessons or drill); and recognizing and valuing the children's early achievements. Above all they help foster interests, inquiry, and positive experiences.

Teachers who have taken to the literature-based aspect of the whole language approach early on, like others who initiate innovative programs, bring with them the enthusiasm which almost guarantees success. Teachers with low expectations for their students have contributed to negative behavior and low achievements from them. Fortunately, the reverse is also true, and teachers' belief in their students performing at exemplary levels will often further that result. Teaching children without the stultifying basals and with the vast array of fine literature for children (much of which is available in paperback format) is an exciting, ever-new, and evolving process.

There has been much criticism of American education as stressing retention of facts and neglecting the higher-level thinking skills such as comparing, contrasting, problem solving, synthesizing, and being able to back up an opinion. Discussing the materials being read, predicting where the plot is going, character analysis, etc., are practices which have been commonplace in secondary school English classes for a long time. The whole language approach played out through literature brings these techniques down to primary grades with different terminology, but with equally interesting and effective results for the students.

2 WHAT THE RESEARCH SAYS: ANSWERS YOU'LL NEED FOR THE TOUGH QUESTIONS

Somehow the experts just cannot seem to agree on the place or value of teaching phonics to young children. In the 1950s Rudolph Flesch challenged the look-say method as not producing good readers (Flesch 1954). He suggested that teaching phonics was the only way to teach reading. In addition, Jeanne Chall's review of research on phonics instruction reiterated the importance of teaching phonics in a sequential way over a look-say method for early and prolonged success in reading (Chall 1967). In fact, her research showed that systematic phonics instruction resulted in success from first through third grades in word recognition, spelling, vocabulary, and reading comprehension. Just when we thought that everyone was fairly secure with the idea that phonics should be a part of early reading instruction, along came the whole language theorists to upset the apple cart again.

In 1965, Ken Goodman did a study to determine how children deal with isolated words in a list as compared with seeing the same words in the context of a story. Using 100 first, second, and third graders as subjects, Goodman exposed the children individually to lists of words taken from a basal reading series not used in their school. After reading the words in isolation, they were asked to read aloud stories containing the same words. Goodman found that all of the children in the study could read in the story at least half of the words they were unable to identify in the list. His conclusions from this study prompted this quote:

> Shotgun teaching of so-called phonic skills to whole classes or groups at the same time seems highly questionable in view of the extreme diversity of the difficulties children displayed in this study (Goodman 1965).

19

Whole language purists in the United States have interpreted these results to mean that phonics should not be taught in any sequential way to young readers. Rather, they suggest that letters and the sounds that correspond to those letters should only be presented when the child expresses a need or desire to know them. This has been one of the most hotly debated issues related to the whole language movement. Because this will be one of the first questions to be asked when presenting the idea of a literature-based program grounded in the whole language philosophy, we will discuss it in some detail here.

Regarding the teaching of phonics, Frank Vellutino states the issue well:

> From a logical standpoint, it seems incontrovertible that learning to read in a writing system based on an alphabet would, of necessity, require that beginning readers become conversant with the alphabetic principle, but this requirement is not acknowledged by most whole language advocates (Vellutino 1991).

The question arises, why do some whole language theorists who accept Goodman's view (and most who come from New Zealand and Australia do *not* support this thinking) tell us repeatedly that language should not be broken down into "bite-size abstract little pieces" (Goodman 1986). Since the teaching of phonics has been traditionally presented in this way, some educators would have teachers eliminate the teaching of phonics in a systematic, sequential way. They feel that it detracts from the practice of immersing the child in a print-rich environment in which words are seen in "whole" contexts rather than in isolation, and that directly exposing children to instruction in letter-to-sound relationships, "tools" they need to deal with unknown words, will reduce their ability to see written language as springing from a "natural" base.

WHAT CURRENT RESEARCH SAYS ABOUT PHONICS INSTRUCTION

In the landmark study of reading instruction in the United States, *Becoming a Nation of Readers*, Anderson and his colleagues addressed this issue. Regarding the issue of phonics instruction, they say:

> What does the research say about the effectiveness of phonics instruction? Classroom research shows that, on the average, children who are taught phonics get off to a better start in reading than children who are not taught phonics (Anderson 1985).

Marilyn Jager Adams, in a new text on beginning reading instruction which is well based on research, tells us that:

> Studies, [on different approaches to beginning reading] suggest that, among broad classes of programs, those that include systematic phonics instruction generally give young readers an edge in spelling and word recognition (Adams 1990).

She states at another point in the book:

> Research reviewed later in the book confirms that letter recognition facility and phonemic awareness are causally related to reading acquisition and that each is a prerequisite for the young child (Adams 1990).

In a replication of Goodman's classic study, Nicholson set out to determine if Goodman's study was affected by order effect. Carried out in New Zealand, there were 100 subjects in this study, six, seven, and eight year olds, who represented a range of poor, average, and good readers. Changing the order in which tasks were done in Goodman's study, Nicholson had one group of subjects first read a passage aloud and then words from the story presented in a list. With another group of subjects, he presented the list of words first and then the oral reading of the story as Goodman had done. His results showed that in the first group the poor readers at six and seven years of age showed significant gains with context while the six, seven, and eight year old average readers showed no reliable gains with context. The good eight year old readers gained significantly with the list. In the second group, the six and seven year old poor readers were unable to cope with the list (context helped but not significantly), significant gains were made only by poor and average older readers. The good six year old readers and the good seven and eight year old readers did not show significant gains. Nicholson comments on his results:

> Results. . .suggest that. . .poor readers rely on context to compensate for their poor decoding skills, whereas good readers, who are good at decoding, have less need to do so (Nicholson 1991).

He further stated that "It appears that the findings of Goodman's [1965] classic study may have exaggerated the effects of context" (Nicholson 1991). In discussing the results of his study, Nicholson tells us that children taught in a whole language approach rely on "enlightened guessing" until they reach a plateau at which they find themselves facing words that are hard to guess. At this point they require the use of decoding skills to help them read words they already know through their listening vocabulary.

In a study which had as its goal to evaluate a new program designed to teach young children about phonological structure, Byrne and Fielding-Barnsley trained 128 preschoolers in their Phonemic Awareness Program. The result:

> . . .strongly supports the hypothesis that, for children four to five years of age, both letter-sound knowledge and phonemic awareness need to be established for acquisition of the alphabetic principle. . .to take place (Byrne & Fielding-Barnsley 1991).

Foorman and her colleagues designed a study to look at the relation among phonemic segmentation, word reading and spelling. They took 83 first graders in lower to middle class schools in Houston, Texas and gave them one of two methods of instruction. One group received a language experience approach with less letter-sound instruction than the other group which learned to sound out and blend in a whole class structured format. In both cases the children were being taught in a basal reading system. They comment in their conclusions:

> The case for the escalating superiority of letter-sound instruction on reading and spelling performance is further supported in the HLM analyses. . .

Later in the section they state:

> . . .it is the segmenting and blending of letter-sound instruction that appears facilitative to the development of reading skill (Foorman et al. 1991).

Ehri and Rubbins performed an interesting study with kindergarten and first grade children in five elementary schools in middle-class northern California. They wanted to look at beginning readers' ability to read new words by analogy. They defined the ability to read words by analogy as reading words that are new to them by relating a known word that is similar in appearance to the new word. They pretested 88 kindergartners and found them to be in two categories, 43 were non-decoders and 45 were considered decoders. They performed a word-training task with the subjects which showed that reading unfamiliar words by analogy is easier than reading unfamiliar words by phonologically recoding them. In addition they concluded that:

> In order for beginners to read words by analogy, they must possess phonological recoding skill. (Ability to analyze spellings into constituent sound units and to blend these units to form a word.) (Ehri & Rubbins, 1992).

In a multilevel study which focused on the issues of teaching reading in ability groups vs. heterogeneously, with trade books vs. with a basal, and with alternative approaches to decoding vs. the approaches presented in basal reading systems, Eldredge and Butterfield worked with 1,149 children whom they divided into experimental and control groups. They used five alternative strategies:

1. Basal reader in homogeneous groups with 10-15 minutes of decoding
2. Basal reader with heterogeneous group using a neurological impress method
3. Basal with heterogeneous grouping using 10-15 minutes of special decoding
4. Literature program
5. Literature program with 10-15 minutes special decoding.

The results of the experiment showed:

> The use of children's literature to teach children to read had a positive effect upon students achievement and attitudes toward reading—much greater than the traditional methods used. . . .The use of special decoding instruction also had a positive effect upon students' achievement and attitudes toward reading—much greater than traditional decoding instruction.

Another comment shared by the experimenters was most interesting. They mentioned that the second graders in the study enjoyed the books they read "despite the lack of vocabulary control and the disregard for sentence length" (Eldredge & Butterfield 1986). In fact, the positive impact upon students' attitude toward reading was mentioned as a byproduct in studies done by Tunnel (1986); Holdaway (1982); Fielding, Wilson, and Anderson (1986); and Eldredge and Butterfield (1986). It seems that this alone would be reason to embrace a literature-based approach since we may safely conclude that if children enjoy reading then they will probably become better readers.

TEACHING SKILLS/PHONICS: WHAT THE EXPERTS SAY

In his book *The Foundations of Literacy*, Holdaway deals with the issue of basic skills instruction directly. He tells us that:

> The danger of analyzing separate skills out from the total task is that they tend to be taught separately, and then used separately. Children gain the misapprehension that they should choose one of the skills and if that doesn't work, try another! It is the integration of skills working together which leads to efficient reading and writing. No single skill can be relied upon to provide a solution which ought to be trusted (Holdaway 1979, 98).

Holdaway suggests that we take the traditional corpus of skills—sight vocabulary, structural analysis, phonics, syllabification, and using context—and add to them the skills of confirmation and self correction. He refers to these as *strategies* which are governed and controlled by the human mind. What he is saying is that by combining instruction in skills with the use of learning strategies the two will work in concert to help the reader during the "search and proposal stages to narrow possibilities into probabilities. . . and render probabilities into near certainties." He also suggests that "the combined skills, working in a strategy, rapidly become automatic or largely so." In other words, if we teach the components of basic skills and set them in the context of strategies, the child will have twice as much ammunition to deal with unknown words. Our goal should be to do this in such a way that the whole process is set into motion very rapidly while the child is reading. Holdaway further states that these three points should be taken into consideration when planning instruction in basic skills:

1. Whatever *skill* is being addressed should be *modeled* by the teacher in the context of a piece of text.
2. The *teaching* of skills should also be done *in* the *context* of wider text because it lends support to the use of the skill being addressed. Seeing words in the context of a larger piece of text also gives the message to the young reader that the *skill/strategy* is to be *used* when they come to an unknown word *as they read* real print. How often have we seen children deal successfully with a sound/symbol relationship in isolation and then be totally baffled when they meet the sound in the context of a sentence. The issue of *transfer of learning* is especially important (Holdaway 1979).

TEACHING GRADES ONE AND TWO

What does all of this mean in the context of classroom planning? Let's look at how one would plan to address skills in the context of a first or second grade literature lesson. If the teacher were planning to expose the children to a specific sound, he or she would plan to introduce it in the context of a Big Book or a poem or chant printed on a piece of large chart paper. For example, if the sound being considered in kindergarten or first grade is "w" the teacher might consider using the Big Book, *Mrs. Wishy Washy*. As the children read the text out loud they will hear the sound of the "w" as they see it in the story. The teacher will call their attention to the sound, ask them for a word in the story that has that has the sound at the beginning, ask them to come up to the the text and frame it with their hands and to say the word out loud. Following this the teacher can have the children give words from their own vocabulary that also begin with the "w" sound. As an extension activity, the children might be asked to find pictures of words or to draw a picture of something that begins with the sound.

Another way of approaching this task is to use what Holdaway calls a *sliding word mask* which focuses the children's attention on specific words in a text to the exclusion of others that stand nearby. It is essentially a piece of cardboard which has a window cut in the center. Another piece of cardboard is positioned behind it in such a way that it can be drawn back and forth to expose parts of words or the whole thing. This type of mask can also be used to reveal whole phrases if they are being discussed. Once the entire text is read out loud by the group, the word containing the sound being addressed that day is highlighted. This tends to be more dramatic than pointing to the word.

Cloze exercises are teaching techniqes that require children to supply missing information. Holdaway suggests that the use of cloze exercises is a good way to deal with sounds instruction and is appropriate in kindergarten, first, and second grades. For example, the children would see a morning message, written beforehand by the teacher, with several words missing their first letters. Through a discussion with the students, possible first letters would be suggested by them. In the case of introducing a sound for the first time, the words chosen should all contain the same first letter/sound. As the year progresses, words containing different first sounds can have their first letters removed as a means of review.

In second grade, the students might be studying homonyms. The teacher could present a poem which contains words that have commonly misinterpreted homonyms printed large enough on a chart for all the children to read. For example, a poem might contain words such as him (hymn), too (to, two), read (reed), their (they're, there). After reading the poem with the group, the teacher will point to the homonyms or underline them and ask the students if they know of any other ways that these words can be spelled, writing them on the board or a piece of chart paper as they are suggested. The teacher would then ask how they know which is the correct one to use, especially when they are using them in their writing, and then might suggest or ask them to offer some other homonyms that are often misinterpreted. Following this the children should have an activity that will allow them to use the homonyms in some way either by writing them in sentences or drawing pictures of objects that represent each word.

If the skill to be addressed is sequencing, a book such as *The Gingerbread Boy*, which comes in many versions, can be used effectively. Following several oral readings, the teacher can do a story map with the children on chart paper or an overhead projector so that it can be brought back the following day. Through discussion of the events in the story, the teacher guides the children to select the main events in the story as she records them. When this has been completed, the children could be asked to make a visual map of the story by drawing pictures of the main events and putting them in order on a large piece of paper. By using real stories instead of worksheets to make the children aware of sequence, we are again helping to bridge the gap between instruction of a skill and transferring the skill to real reading situations.

DEVELOPING SIGHT VOCABULARY

Teaching sight vocabulary is best done through a shared-reading activity. In the shared-reading activity we are attempting to replicate the reading that was done by the parents or caregivers when the children were younger. With the text visible to all, the parents read the story out loud as the children followed along with their eyes. After several readings of a favorite story, the children would often be able to repeat several parts on their own. There would also be times when the parents might point out certain features of words or favorite phrases with which the children have become enchanted.

In the classroom setting, Big Books are used in a similar way. The text is large enough to be seen by a whole group of children. The teacher gathers the entire class and reads the text of the story out loud several times. When the children feel comfortable with most of the words in the story, they will begin to chime in with words they know. Those who are still unsure will continue to listen until they can identify the words on sight. This is done in a very nonthreatening way and allows the children to develop sight vocabulary at their own individual pace. Unlike the traditional "round robin" strategy where children were expected to perform even when they were unsure of words, this method allows for maximum comfort for the young beginning reader. It is amazing to see how many words children pick up using the shared reading technique; certainly more words are learned this way than by using word cards containing words they would memorize out of context.

In a book filled with strategies for use in the literature-based classroom, Johnson and Louis (1987) offer these suggestions for developing sight vocabulary:

If the nursery rhyme "Ding Dong Bell" is being presented,

Ding Dong Bell,
Pussy's in the well.
Who put her in?
Little Tommy Thin.
Who'll pull her out?
Little Johnny Stout.

the teacher might highlight familiar words, phrases or lines in two ways:

1. Frame a familiar word, phrase, or line (with hands or a ruler) and say, "This line says 'Ding Dong Bell.' "
2. Frame the line and ask, "What does this line say?" (Pussy's in the well.)

Or the teacher might point out familiar words by saying "This is Tommy" and then ask the children to find words or phrases by saying "Where does it say 'pull'?" or "Where does it say 'Little Tommy'?"

Another technique that Johnson and Louis recommend for sight vocabulary development is to print out on cards the phrases to a nursery rhyme such as:

Hickory, dickory, dock.
The mouse ran / up the clock.
The clock / struck one,
The mouse / ran down,
Hickory, dickory, dock.

Johnson and Louis also suggest that phrases that begin lines should be done before those that end lines (hence the slashes in the middle lines). With the copy of the entire text of the nursery rhyme on a large sheet of chart paper, a card would be given to a child to match to the same phrase in the rhyme. It is important to mention that the children should have a familiarity with the rhyme before this task is done.

A similar type of exercise can be done to further sight vocabulary. Called a progressive cloze technique, this requires that all the words of a nursery rhyme or poem be printed on separate cards and displayed in a pocket chart (there are pocket charts made of a clear plastic which allow the cards to be seen without difficulty) or on a flannel board. After a rhyme such as

> Jack be nimble,
> Jack be quick,
> Jack jump over
> The candlestick

has been read in its entirety several times so that the children have a good sense of the words, some of the words are removed one or two at a time.

> Jack be _____,
> Jack be _____,
> Jack jump _____
> The candlestick.

The children would then say the rhyme or poem over again and supply the missing word which would then be returned to its original position. The words would be progressively eliminated until only the structure words were visible. It must be reiterated at this point that the children must know the poem or rhyme well before this strategy is used.

The reverse of this procedure is the regressive cloze. The entire text of the rhyme or poem is shown. Then all but the structure words are removed such as:

> _____ be _____,
> _____ be _____,
> _____ _____ over
> The _____.

The children are asked to supply the missing words which are returned to their correct position as the rhyme is recited (Johnson and Louis 1987).

There are a number of suggestions in Johnson and Louis' book about skills development. In addition to ideas for phonics and word structure development, they also have ideas about how to extend children's appreciation of books that are more exciting than the traditional book report. For example, they talk about literary report cards, literary passports, literary posters, journals, literary sociograms, plot profiles, and literary interviews. This is a text worth looking at.

BUILDING CONFIDENCE

Regarding the question of sight word development, it is important at this point to refer back to Holdaway's reference to the "search and proposal stages of reading" which we mentioned earlier. The question often arises as to what we should do when children are reading orally and come to a word that they do not know. In his book *Independence in Reading,* Holdaway mentions that:

> The outstanding characteristic of retarded and reluctant readers is their dependence on others for both help and assurance. They develop a remarkable range of techniques to wrest aid from those who are unwilling to give it (Holdaway 1980, 67).

What Holdaway suggests is to ask a series of questions, rather than supply an unknown word for the child, which will help them become less dependent on adults. For example, rather than say "What is this word?" we might say "Is this word _____?" If the reply is "no," we might ask how the child knows that. In this way we are helping children to become aware of the things they do know about words. With practice, they will come to employ them on a regular basis. Independence is the key word here. If we fail to develop self-checking strategies we are paralyzing the child as a reader rather than building his or her independence. Holdaway tells us to refer to children's sense of language as it is spoken. If they read something out loud that does not ring true, we can ask "Does that sound right, is that the way people talk?" When they learn to think that way often enough, guided by our questions, the same pattern will develop internally so that the questions will be asked automatically whenever they come to an unknown word. We must remind them that they know certain phonic elements and that the time has come to use them. Otherwise our function as facilitator of language development is diminished.

What we have attempted to do here is give some idea about how skills can be developed in a sequential way without resorting to isolated, drill-like instruction. It is a major issue related to developing a literature-based reading program and addressing it adequately could take volumes. We have attempted to share some insights and refer to other sources which deal with this topic in greater detail than can be done here. Our main focus is to emphasize the idea that skills can be successfully addressed in a literature-based reading program and can be addressed in such a way that they will become an integral part of the young reader's growth as a literate person.

3 HOW TO LIGHT THE FIRE: PROMOTING INTEREST

Form a Language Arts Committee

Now the real fun begins. All the hard work has been done—the "powers that be" are convinced that a literature-based reading program is not only worthwhile but will imbue children with a desire to read. The next step is to take the idea to the teachers who will implement it. In some cases this will require little effort. In other cases, however, it will be a monumental task. How do you convince people that what you want them to do is educationally beneficial for the children even though it will require them to expend a great deal of time and effort, two commodities stretched to the limit in the life of today's classroom teacher?

Without doubt, the library media specialist and the reading specialist in each school must collaborate if success is hoped for in the development of the literature-based program. This collaboration must be initiated from the beginning of the process and must continue throughout the life of the program. A division of labor or a splintering of philosophy will severely jeopardize the growth of the program. When you think about it, it simply makes a lot of sense to draw connections between the two providers of literature instruction whose contributions can be compared to two sides of the same coin, and for them to join forces.

THE GAME PLAN UNFOLDS

If teachers are expected to enthusiastically embrace the movement toward a literature-based reading program, it is very important that they be involved in the process from the start. One good way is to form a group to direct the movement. We suggest the formation of a Language Arts Committee consisting of teachers from each grade level, reading consultants/specialists, and the language arts supervisor if there is one in the district. When forming the Language Arts Committee, whether in-house or district-wide, the library media

33

specialist should be invited to join. Since this will be the policy-forming group for language arts, it is important to have input from the librarian regarding selection of titles and purchase of materials for the program. For example, even though it is suggested that teachers make selections of trade book titles to be used at their grade level, recommendations from the library media specialist should be expected and encouraged. Just as school librarians are prepared to give book talks to students in the classrooms, so should they be encouraged to do the same for faculty members.

The library media specialists in our schools have a wealth of knowledge and too often much of it is lost or taken for granted. Not only are they aware of more efficient and cost-saving ways to purchase and process literature titles, they also have a greater knowledge of children's literature than many classroom teachers. Most important, school librarians in quality schools have teacher certification and are fully versed in curriculum development and learning theory. Also, they generally keep abreast of the most recent titles on the market and can alert faculty to new and promising titles and those that should be avoided in spite of how well they are promoted. This can save a great deal of time, effort, and money in the long run since books that are purchased for the literature-based collection should be obtained with an eye to cost saving if possible. Therefore, we are suggesting not only that the library media specialist be a member of the Language Arts Committee, we are also recommending that she or he participate in the grade-level selection of titles.

The Language Arts Committee would operate as an advisory group and joining would be voluntary. Its primary function would be to make recommendations to the superintendent regarding the reading and language arts program. It is advisable to meet at least once a month because there will be several issues related to the reading program that will surface during the period of its development that will require immediate attention. There are a few points to mention regarding committee meetings:

1. Be sure that there is an agenda for the meeting. It is helpful to get it to committee members ahead of time but, if that is not possible, it should be presented at the beginning of the meeting in either oral or written form.
2. The committee chairperson should be present when committee members arrive at the meeting place. This

maneuver is recommended because it helps to reduce the amount of negative conversation that can develop while people are waiting for the meeting to begin.

3. Keep minutes of the meetings and have them typed and distributed to the members. You will be surprised at how many times you will refer to them when you are reviewing decisions and/or recommendations.

4. Serve refreshments at the meetings. After a full day of teaching, teachers need a little lift. It will keep them on task much longer than if you forego it.

5. Set a definite time for adjourning the meeting and stick to it as closely as possible. You will find that people concentrate on the issues more closely if they know that the meeting has a definite closing time.

At the very beginning, someone should persuade the upper-level administrators who have given the go-ahead to the movement to allow things to develop at a pace that is comfortable for all concerned, especially the classroom teachers who will bring literature-based reading to life. This is vital to success and cannot be stressed enough. Just as whole language theorists remind us to respect the development of the child, so must we respect the adults who work with these children allowing them to move into this at their own pace. Since the basal reading approach has dominated reading instruction for so many years, most classroom teachers will have used it as the method of instruction, totally or in part, depending on their own professional preferences or the requirements of the school system in which they work. If this support, with which they have become comfortable, is removed before they are ready to act on their own, the new, alternative program will be doomed from the start. This point is integral to the success of the program and will be reiterated in the chapters that follow.

WORKSHOPS TO CREATE A KNOWLEDGE BASE

This book began with two chapters designed to provide the busy administrator and/or the reading professional with a knowledge base which they could use as ammunition of sorts. Before teachers can make a decision about whether or not a literature-based reading program is better than a basal system, they also must be given the opportunity to understand what it is. In knowledge there is strength. Therefore, the first step in the process is to provide workshops on the theory behind the whole language/literature-based movement.

Naturally, the first question will be where to find people who will speak on this topic. In most cases, the reading professionals will have access to the names of speakers through their local or state professional reading organizations. If that does not yield fruit, these national organizations should be contacted:

The International Reading Association
800 Barksdale Rd.
PO Box 8139
Newark, DE 19714-8139
302-731-1600

The National Council of Teachers of English
1111 Kenyon Rd.
Urbana, IL 61801
217-328-3870

Both of these organizations would be able to supply contacts within state and local affiliates of I.R.A. which in turn could provide names of presenters who reside close to the area of the school district. Another organization that is fairly new to the scene but which is gaining momentum is TAWL (Teachers Applying Whole Language). A national address is not yet available, but watch for flyers that do come in about their workshops. Staff at one of the associations named above should know someone active in the movement, as should reading department personnel at the nearest university.

In addition to getting the information that these organizations provide about speakers, it is also advisable to join them as professional members. In most cases, membership provides information about local and statewide workshops and conferences where a good number of the best presenters give talks and workshops. These organizations also send flyers to central office personnel about upcoming conferences. If you are moving into literature-based reading at the school building level only, a call to the district supervisor or curriculum director is advisable.

Another good source of information is the state education department. In many instances their reading and language arts personnel people will not only provide the names of good presenters, they are also available to work with districts who wish to move in this direction. It is not a bad idea to request of them an evaluation of your present program. This evaluation can function as a stepping stone into a literature-based program. In addition, some state education departments offer workshops and/or retreats for school district personnel who are seriously exploring the possibility of moving away from a basal program. Central office personnel should be contacted to inquire about these points.

School districts should also begin to build up a professional library as a part of the library media center, in each school building, which would lend books related to literature-based programs and the whole language movement to teachers. Journals and articles should also be available to teachers for their perusal.

Opportunities for teachers to attend workshops and conferences where reading and language arts topics are discussed are a must. The more opportunities classroom teachers and reading and library specialists have to hear and experience the philosophy and realities of a literature-based program from professionals who are doing it, the greater will be their willingness to try it. If they know it has been instituted, that it does have a positive effect on children and that with determination and support it does come together, then they will come into it with a less fearful frame of mind.

ORGANIZE YOUR WORKSHOPS

How you proceed with this phase will make all the difference between a successful beginning and a rocky one. Up to this point, most of the work you have completed has been done by your own people working in a quiet but steady manner. When you plan a workshop, in a sense you are going public with the philosophy of the movement. Except for your presentation of the action plan to the faculty, there has heretofore been no opportunity for the teachers to interact with the precepts of the literature-based program.

The choice of presenters who will give the workshops should be carefully made. Keep in mind that at the early stages of development not every teacher and administrator in the district will favor a move away from basal reading instruction. Therefore, the person or persons who come to talk about this topic should be individuals who will have high credibility. They must be able to convince their audience that they can identify in some way with their roles as classroom teachers and/or administrators. Ideally, bringing in presenters who are classroom teachers, reading administrators, or principals who have been through this kind of change would answer this need nicely. However, this is not always possible especially if workshops are held during the school day when these people are involved with their own district responsibilities.

Suffice it to say that the presenters chosen should have had some connection with school district reading programs that have been or are undergoing change. It will be their job to marry the theory with practice in some sort of exciting format. If you are forced to bring in university personnel, try to choose people who have had some fairly recent experience with school systems, even if it is limited to their involvement as consultants in a school district on an ongoing basis. While all of this seems to be minor, getting your campaign off on a sour note by bringing in a presenter who alienates the faculty can have as damaging an effect on the process as choosing the wrong topic for the introductory workshop.

When you bring in workshop presenters, faculty members will have a chance to listen, to think, to ask questions, to react. There is every possibility (even probability) that some degree of negativity will surface at this point. When people are fearful of change, this is not an uncommon response. What you want to guard against is allowing that negativity to dominate the atmosphere. To prevent this from happening, you must carefully decide what your opening topic should be. For the first workshop, we suggest that you consider focusing on the changes that are current in reading instruction. The presenters should give practical examples of some new strategies that could be used in the classroom to foster comprehension and study skills development. The strategies should be appropriate for primary and intermediate students and should be presented in such a way that they could be used the next day in the classroom without any more preparation than has been given in the workshop. The teachers should have a taste of something that is new but has practical application in their classrooms. At this point there should be no real discussion of the components of literature-based reading programs. The purpose is to give the teachers a sense that things that are new are not necessarily bad or problematic. They can even use the strategies with their basal reading lessons. Make sure that they leave the workshop with a clear idea about how to use the strategy and then let them go. You will be surprised how many of them try the new ideas in the classroom. If they are allowed the freedom to choose whether or not to do it and when, they will be more open to the changes that you will present later.

Following this first workshop, bring in presenters who are doing literature-based programs in their school systems. Have a workshop for the primary teachers and one for the intermediate teachers. The presenters should give very practical ideas about how to implement this kind of program in the classrooms. Teachers should be given some ideas to try in their reading classes. The difference here is in the more focused nature of the presentations. Both of these workshops may be given in the spring so that teachers can use the information to plan their programs during the summer months if they so desire.

TAKE A GIANT STEP: SIT DOWN TOGETHER AND THINK

There isn't a classroom teacher worth his or her salt who doesn't realize the value and importance of planning for instruction. Many educators have seen worthwhile projects fail because there was too little time given to planning.

The first phase in planning is to draw up an action plan. If the state education department or its regional resource centers do offer assistance in the form of curriculum retreats, this is a highly desirable way to move. If such a service does not exist, a school district might consider holding its own retreat.

A curriculum retreat is an opportunity for district educators to remove themselves from the hustle and bustle of daily school life in order to concentrate exclusively on the task of creating an "action plan" for moving into a literature-based reading program. In its purest form, a retreat suggests that the participants physically remove themselves from the workplace and from all their responsibilities and spend approximately three days together, including evenings, thrashing out their beliefs about reading/language arts instruction. Under the direction of a trained facilitator, the strengths and weaknesses of the district's reading program would be examined, priorities for improvement would be explored, possible options would be considered, and an action plan would be created.

Who would be invited to participate in such a retreat? There should be a representative from the administrative level and several representatives from the faculty. The Connecticut

State Department of Education has sponsored such retreats and recommends that the team consist of from five to eight individuals, an administrator (central office), a principal, and teachers. At least one teacher from each academic level (primary and middle school), a reading consultant, and a school librarian should be invited to participate. If the district has a language arts committee, the members should have the first opportunity to attend since they have given evidence of their commitment to improving language arts instruction by their contribution of time to committee work. (Should committee members be unable to participate, the invitation should then be extended to district teachers.) If, however, such a committee does not exist, it is advisable to form one as soon as consideration is given to changing or expanding the district's reading/language arts program. The committee allows teachers to participate actively in the change process. The Language Arts Committee would formulate and present recommendations related to language arts instruction to the superintendent and the board of education.

The first step in the retreat process is information analysis (Institute for Teaching and Learning (I.T.L.) 1987). In order to do that, information about the present program has to be gathered. This information would include any recently completed evaluations of the reading/language arts program, student testing results, and results of questionnaires which should be given to students, faculty members, administrators, and parents. The information gleaned from such surveys should reflect the impressions of the entire school population, including teachers, students, parents, and administrators, about the reading/language arts program. It will be useful only to the extent that it tells the district personnel how the program has been running and what each segment of the school population would like to see happen to make it better. Such a focus, if properly executed, will have a great impact upon the development of an action plan. The questionnaires should therefore be focused, realistic, and open to criticism, both positive and negative. There should be no attempt to formulate questions in such a way as to control or restrain the responses.

THE "TAKE ACTION" PLAN

When the participants arrive at the retreat location, their first task will be to take the information they have gathered and set about writing an issue statement. This statement should reflect the problem or "issue" to be resolved through action. The statement *should not suggest a solution*, it should merely state the reason why action must occur. It should indicate what kind of issue exists, who is affected, and what is the source of the issue (I.T.L. 1987). For example:

> *Issue Statement: The students in our district do not have a love of reading for pleasure. In addition, they are not comprehending what they read at an inferential and critical level of thinking. It appears that reading, as it is taught to them through the basal reading system, is unexciting and results in their functioning at a very low level of thought.*

While this statement offers two issues to be dealt with, they are essentially two sides of the same coin. (It is important that this be kept in mind. One issue statement should not contain two issues that each beg for a different solution.) In this case the problems look for a single solution which will in some way resolve both situations.

Once the issue statement has been completed, action objectives must be developed to respond to needs identified. These objectives give direction to the program that will be put in place:

> *Action Objective: By June, a plan will be in place to provide teachers with information, techniques, and resources for implementing a literature-based approach to reading instruction.*

Such a goal must be realistic enough to be accepted by both the teachers and administrators who will be asked to implement it. It also has an open-ended quality to it in the sense that it does not confine the practitioners to certain movements while excluding others.

Before developing an action plan, it is important to reflect not only on the strategies to be presented, but how those strategies will be accepted by the faculty. It is much better to determine where "the land mines" are before taking the group across the field so that as many casualties as possible can be prevented. In other words, *plan ahead*. Examples of questions that we came up with follow:

1. Is the movement we are taking in line with current research?
2. Will it be best to have a variety of presentations or one major speaker?
3. Will there be much opposition from faculty members?
4. Is this going to mean a greater work overload for the teachers?
5. Do we have the time, finances, people, and materials needed to do the job right?

As the action plan is developed, these questions should be addressed.

At this point the action plan should be developed. The action plan will address each step to be taken, what date it will be executed, what is the anticipated date of completion, who is responsible for each step, and what evidence will be needed to show that the action has been completed. An example of part of an action plan is listed here:

Step 1: The retreat committee will meet with the superintendent to share the results of the action plan.

Person responsible: Retreat committee chair.

Timeline: Within three weeks after the retreat.

Evidence of accomplishment: The meeting will have occurred.

Step 2: Inform the Language Arts Committee of the results of the retreat.

Person responsible: Language Arts Supervisor.

Timeline: Within one week after meeting with the superintendent.

Evidence of accomplishment: Language Arts Committee minutes will reflect that the retreat was discussed.

Step 3: Inform the faculty of the results of the retreat. Share with them the action plan.

> *Person responsible*: Retreat committee chair or designate.

> *Timeline*: Within a month of the meeting with the superintendent.

> *Evidence of accomplishment*: Meeting will have occurred.

Step 4: Determine budget allocations.

> *Person responsible*: The superintendent in conjunction with the retreat committee.

> *Timeline:* By the end of January.

> *Evidence of accomplishment*: Budget approved by the Board of Education.

Step 5: Plan for workshops.

> *Person responsible*: Language Arts Supervisor in conjunction with the Language Arts Committee.

> *Timeline*: Sometime in the spring.

> *Evidence of Accomplishment*: Workshops presented.

Each step in the action plan should relate to the action objective developed by the district. It should be sequential and complete. The action plan will provide direction to whatever movement the district takes regarding an area of the curriculum, in this case literature-based reading.

Following the development of the steps to be taken, it is advisable to consider the resources needed to accomplish the plan, the constraints that might be encountered along the way, and what evaluation criteria will be used somewhere along the way as the district moves ahead (I.T.L. 1987).

At this point a caveat about resources is in order. Often-times educators will make decisions about curriculum development on the basis of money. In the case of literature-based reading programs, the thought of having to purchase a raft of new literature titles can cause paralysis. Reiterating what was said earlier, it is best to go slowly rather than push ahead with a vengeance. The library media specialist, fully involved, may have invaluable strategies and insights to offer. When we discuss selecting titles, we will address this issue in more detail. There are some valuable points to consider in conjunction with this topic which could make a difference between going ahead and stopping dead in one's tracks.

WHAT TO DO NEXT

After the faculty has been informed of the "what," the "wherefore," and the "how" of the process and have had a chance to hear some quality presentations on the topic of literature-based reading and the current changes in reading instruction, it will be time to involve them in some activities that will get the ball rolling.

One of the first steps to take will be to visit school districts that have existing literature-based reading programs or at least are in the process of moving in that direction. This is important because it gives you a chance to see the process in action and to ask a lot of questions. It will help you to find the best way to proceed and also to avoid many pitfalls. In the end, it should prove to be a very profitable experience.

When you have decided to visit other districts, the next step is to find out where they are. There are a number of ways to do this. The first place to check is with the reading personnel in your district. Because many of them belong to professional reading organizations, they will have contacts in other school districts as a result of this association. The same applies to the school librarian on your own Language Arts Committee or others. Use their knowledge. Another possibility is to contact state department consultants. They move throughout the state visiting school districts. In fact, they may also have worked with the types of districts for which you are searching. If these steps fail to get you contacts, which is highly unlikely, grab the state school district directory and call district curriculum directors or supervisors to find out what kind of programs they have in their schools. You may find that other districts are also looking for the same information. This might lead to some future collaboration.

Before making any visits, it will be important to sit down with the visiting teams and chart out your course in terms of what you will be looking for and what specific questions you would like to have answered. In particular, you should consider these points:

1. How did they replace the basal? Was the move gradual or swift?
2. How is instruction in skills development addressed? Are there workbooks and/or worksheets used?
3. Were teachers given assistance as they moved ahead? What kind of help was offered?
4. How did they decide on the titles that would be used in the literature-based program? How much involvement did the teachers have in the process? Did they rely on the school librarian's knowledge not only of material but of teaching and learning?
5. How did they finance the purchases?
6. What part did the school librarians in the district play in the development of the program?
7. Was the reading curriculum revised before beginning?
8. Who gave the teachers guidance in the development of lessons for the literature texts?
9. Do they have a Language Arts Committee? If not, how were decisions made as they developed the program?
10. How did they inform parents of the changes taking place?
11. How did they present the ideas to the superintendent and Board of Education members?

In addition to these and other questions, the team should have in mind certain points they will look for when they visit the school. Having asked to visit classrooms to see literature lessons, team members should look for certain things. For example, during a visit to the school library media center, book-related activities should be apparent. Since the activities going on at the primary and intermediate levels can vary significantly due to the different focuses in instruction, consider the following points when visiting classrooms.

Primary Level (K-3)

1. How does the teacher introduce a Big Book to the group? Is there discussion about the pictures and the words on the cover? Does the teacher try to make connections between the topic of the book and the children's own experiences? Is the book read to the children first? Do they listen as the teacher reads?
2. If the teacher is introducing a trade (library) book, how is it presented to the class? Is there discussion similar to that which takes place when a Big Book is introduced?
3. How is skills instruction carried on? Does the teacher use the text to focus on skills or is it done in isolation? How many skills are addressed in one lesson?
4. What kinds of questions does the teacher ask during the lesson? Do the students have challenging ideas to think about?
5. What kind of follow-up activities does the teacher suggest? Do they seem to be tied into something that was discussed in the story or to a skill that was presented? Do they seem to be creative or more like workbook activities?
6. Is there evidence of writing activities tied into reading lessons?
7. In looking about the room, does there appear to be evidence of involvement in developing themes or topics?
8. How do the children react to the reading lesson? Do they appear excited and involved in a positive way?

Middle School Level (4-8)

1. Are there *prereading* activities such as discussions about vocabulary or attempts to engage the students' background knowledge about the setting or characters in the story? Is there an attempt to fill in pieces of background information that are missing in the students' experience? If so how does the teacher do this?
2. As the students read from the text, what kinds of *questions* does the teacher ask at the conclusion of

their reading? How do the students react to the questions? Is there lively discussion or does it appear to be stilted as if the teacher expects specific answers? Are the questions mostly literal in nature or is there a good mixture of inferential, critical and creative questions in addition to the literal?

3. Does there appear to be any skills instruction going on as the teacher is checking for comprehension? For example, was the focus on antonyms, colorful language, character development, setting, or any number of other possibilities? Do the students learn from the text or is the instruction separated from a reference to the story? Are worksheets used? Do they appear to be of good quality?

4. Does the teacher assign any extension activities? What is the nature of these activities? Do they appear to have as their purpose strengthening the students' understanding of a particular concept brought up in discussion or increasing their knowledge of points made in the story? Do they seem worthwhile or do they appear to be "busy work"?

5. Is there evidence in the classroom of integration of reading and writing into other content areas? For example, are there projects by the students in which reading research and writing are evident?

6. As the students are engaged in reading discussions or extension activities? As they are writing, do they seem to be very involved in the activities to the extent that there are few discipline problems? Do they look as though they are enjoying themselves?

When the visiting teams have returned to the district, they should sit with the Language Arts Committee and share their findings. As a matter of fact, it should be a prerequisite of their going that they will report to that committee. This is important because it is the language arts committee that will be making recommendations to the superintendent and the Board of Education regarding the literature-based program. In order for their recommendations to bear weight, they will have to be well grounded in research. A visit to another school district should be considered field or action research. Therefore, the results of the visits must be shared.

LAUNCHING YOUR PROGRAM

Once all this groundwork has been laid, the process of deciding which books to use in the literature program begins. This is a crucial point in the process and should be done with great care. A very complete discussion of this process will be given in chapter 4. However, it is important to mention here that the teachers who use the books should have the direct first-hand experience in choosing titles. This would be done with the assistance of the school librarian. Regrettably, not every public school is fortunate enough to have such a valuable resource person. If that is the case in your district, it will be especially important for the teachers to follow the suggestions given in chapter 4 regarding how to determine the types of books for your program. The point to be made here is one that has been stressed throughout this book: teachers will buy into the program only if they become part of the process, if they have ownership. You might well seek consultant assistance of an excellent school librarian from a nearby district.

GETTING YOUR FEET WET

Now is the time to let some book movement begin. Of course, the materials must be present when the teachers come back in September if anything is to get started. So it will be very important for the library media specialist to work closely with school personnel to assure that the books have been ordered and processed by the end of August. If you have spent a good part of the late winter and early spring months preparing teachers for this teaching/learning adventure, it is very likely that they will spend a good part of the summer reading the books and, hopefully, getting excited about the possibility of trying the program. If they come back to school and find that the trade books are not available for their use, they will lose their enthusiasm and retreat to the comfort of the old familiar basal. It is not necessary to have every trade book on the designated titles list available but you should have enough titles ready so that those who are ready to go will have a good selection.

The first question to consider will be: What is the best way to proceed? If you have accepted the premise that a slow, steady pace will assure success, then the decisions you make about implementation will reflect that position. We did accept this principle and it had a positive influence on the development of our program. In the beginning the teachers were told that they could move into the use of literature at the rate that was most comfortable for them. They could move into it completely and replace the use of the basal text with trade books. Some teachers chose to try a complete story book with one of their reading groups while keeping the other students in the basal. Other lower grade teachers decided to do the basal program three days a week and to spend two days using literature-based materials. Some first, second, and third grade teachers still used a basal text, a workbook, and the basal teacher's manual to guide them in skills development while using the trade books in a supplemental fashion. Almost every teacher continued to use the skills workbook during the first year. End-of-unit/end-of book tests tied into the basal series were used throughout the first three years. This was done because redesigning reading assessment would be such a monumental task that having the program well in place before deciding how to assess the children was considered the best method of attack. Assessment will be discussed in more detail later in the book.

Before teachers use their first trade book, try to hold a grade level team meeting to talk about developing a literature lesson. A format should be presented to team members along with a literature lesson that has been developed for one of the books on their list. Discuss how the lesson is to be developed as well as proper questioning strategies. Give a copy of the lesson to each teacher for his or her sample lessons binder. Before the conclusion of the first meeting, each teacher on the team should choose one title to prepare for a literature lesson. Hold a team meeting each month that follows, at which team members present their literature lessons. At that time, other team members may offer suggestions for additional extension activities that could be used in conjunction with the book. Following this, type the lesson with the extension activities and make copies for team members to place in their literature binder.

As the year moves along, the teachers will try the lessons with their students and will return to the team meetings with assessments of how well things are working. One of the nice by-products of these meetings will be the discussions about literature that ensue in a very natural way. Talking about children's books generates an enthusiasm for teaching the literature lessons. As the teachers use the lessons, their fears about the program slowly fade. These monthly meetings also give the teachers the opportunity to hear positive and negative points about the books in terms of how well they are or are not being received by the children. In some cases, two teachers using the same book with their respective classes will have totally opposite experiences. This will serve to point out a lesson all can benefit from, namely, that you cannot always predict how a group will react to a book. Also, you will begin to see that some books do well with students of varying ability in reading, while others can only be used successfully with children of either strong or weak skills. These are the kinds of lessons that are learned as the district moves through the process and they cannot always be predicted beforehand.

DEVELOPING A LITERATURE LESSON

There are a number of possible ways to develop a literature lesson. What is presented here is a suggestion. Before giving the specifics of how to go about it, a few caveats should be mentioned. First, the purpose in doing this exercise with the teachers is not to accumulate a raft of literature lessons in much the same way that teachers' manuals are developed. Rather, it is intended to give teachers the practice in how to do it. After the first year we did not go any further with it. Second, there is the possibility in developing these lessons that so much effort will be given to analyzing the book that it will lose its appeal for the students. Therefore, moderation is suggested both in preparing lessons and in implementing them. Because trade books are a rich source of language and lend themselves so nicely to skills development, it is sometimes hard to resist the temptation to get as much out of the book as possible. However, one of our primary goals in all of this continues to be to make reading an enjoyable process for the children. If we over-analyze books, students will come to see reading as a taxing process and trade books as boring material.

THE STORY MAP

When you prepare a literature lesson at the K-3 levels we suggest that you start with a story map. This allows you to see the structure of the story in synopsis form. (The longer books at the 4-6 grade levels do not lend themselves to such abbreviated analysis.) The components of the story map are suggested by Beck and her associates (Beck, et al. 1979).

Basically, the story map uses the structure of a story which consists of:

Title:
Author:
Setting:
    Place:
    Time:
    Major Characters:

Problem: (What is the major problem that the main character has to deal with in the story?)

Goal: (What does the main character have to do to resolve the problem?)

Events: (List the major events that show the main character trying to achieve his or her goal.)

Resolution: (The point in the story when the problem is resolved.)

PREREADING

Following the development of the story map, the core of the lesson is prepared. There are three phases to the literature lesson:

- The prereading section,
- The reading section, and
- The post reading section.

In the prereading section activities are suggested that will acquaint the students with information about the setting of the story or the characters or knowledge that will help them to understand the events in the story. It is at this phase that background knowledge is assessed or laid, depending on the awareness level of the group. The prereading exercises can be any type of activity from reading to the children, discussion of vocabulary words integral to the story (always done in the context of the story), watching a movie related to the topic, to direct instruction or discussion about concepts or authors or setting. The important thing to remember here is that the teacher must convey an enthusiasm for the book if the children are to become excited about it. Macon and his colleagues refer to this phase of the reading process as "engagement."

This is a good choice of words because it creates an image of student participation rather than passivity. So the teacher should plan prereading activities that by their very nature are stimulating. What follows are some suggestions. Some of these activities can take place in the school library with the teacher and the librarian working as a team.

1. Oftentimes teachers will pose questions to be answered later in the story as the events unfold. This helps readers to keep alert to incidents and characters.
2. Another worthwhile activity is to have the students make predictions about what they think is going to happen in the first few pages of the story. Write their predictions on the board or, better yet, on a large piece of poster paper or overhead projector sheet. Then have the students read the pages, check the accuracy of their predictions and make new ones. This can be done throughout the book.
3. A discussion of the author can be held as a prereading activity. This is especially interesting if the book is written by an author that the students are familiar with through prior exposure. This lends itself to a study of the author's treatment of character, plot, description, etc.
4. If there are scientific or social studies concepts to be discussed in the story or book which might be unfamiliar to the students, prereading time might be spent presenting the information in some hands-on experimental format.
5. As mentioned previously, reading to the children can be a prereading activity. Something from the book itself can be read or a piece from another work that relates in some way to the present work can be given.

The possibilities for prereading activities are endless and are limited only by the imagination of the teacher. It is important to remember that the activity should create an interest in the book and excite the reader.

READING

The second phase of the literature lesson is the reading portion. During this phase the reader will do the reading and will join the other students afterwards in a discussion. The teacher might also use this opportunity to address some skills.

It is highly desirable to have the reading done in school to assure that it has been done. Nothing is more frustrating to a teacher than to have a portion of the group fail to read the story which has been assigned as homework. In addition, it promotes a theory that has long been ignored, namely, that it is acceptable to spend instructional time in silent reading. The amount of reading to be done depends upon the length and structure of the book. For example, if it is a book used at the primary level, chances are that it is fairly short. In this case, the teacher would divide the story into sections which would be marked at strategic points for discussion. If it is a chapter book, the natural place to stop would be at the end of a chapter. This is not sacrosanct, however. Two or three chapters can be read before a discussion is held.

At this point, consideration must be given to the subject of discussion of the text. The following points related to discussion bear consideration:

> Discussion is an integral part of a quality reading program, especially when it is literature-based. When students are engaged in a lively discussion of a literature selection, their *comprehension* of that selection is greatly enhanced, not only through thoughtful questions posed by the teacher but also through interaction with other students in the discussion process (Macon, et al. 1989).

The following list paraphrases suggestions given by Macon and his colleagues:

1. The teacher functions as a facilitator or orchestrator during the discussion and keeps the dialogue moving and on task with a lot of interaction.
2. While the teacher would have a list of prepared questions to work from, he or she should be open to formulating new questions that arise from issues raised through discussion.
3. All levels of thinking should be focused on during discussion and the teacher's questions should be formulated to address these levels.
4. While discussion groups can vary in size, it is not desirable to allow them to become larger than 12. (At

the lower grades groups of eight to ten should be considered maximum for very able readers and fewer for less capable readers.)

5. The importance of providing "wait time" of five or more seconds after each question cannot be stressed enough. This will give the more thoughtful, slower thinkers, who often have deep insights to offer, a chance to be heard.

6. If conflicts arise about the responses to literal, fact-level questions, the students should be sent back to the text to verify their answers.

7. All students should be brought into the discussion in one way or another.

8. The teacher's reactions to the students' responses should be carefully monitored. The teacher's role is to keep the dialogue moving. Negative reactions to responses given by students or indicating that there is an expected answer should be avoided at all costs. (Macon, et al. 1989).

It is important to mention at this point that one should avoid the temptation to assign questions to the students for their written responses as was often done in the basal series to "check for comprehension." This will quickly kill enthusiasm for the book. It is acceptable, however, to give a question at the conclusion of the discussion period which they might respond to in writing as a homework assignment. Often such assignments are the springboard to an exciting discussion the next day. The question, however, should be of a creative nature rather than one designed to find out if they understood what they read.

Finally, discussion of a book is vitally important in emphasizing the social aspect of reading, the sharing that leads to common ground and negates the concept of reading as the isolated activity of loners.

DEVELOPMENT OF SKILLS

In addition to discussion of the events or characters in the story, the text can and should be used to highlight *development of skills*. It doesn't matter whether the skills to be addressed are in phonics, vocabulary, or comprehension strategies. It is always desirable to use the words or phrases that are set in the context of rich language as a starting point. Proceeding in this way has two advantages. First, the quality of the text (presuming, of course, that the story is well written) heightens the child's awareness of how well-written text conveys meaning. Second, seeing words or phrases in the context of a story or nonfiction piece, rather than in isolation, fixes in the child's mind the idea that transferring the strategy to real-life reading is the reason for studying the strategy in the first place. Oftentimes, students will do fine when studying the skill in isolation and then practicing it on a worksheet. However, when it comes to applying it in a real-life reading situation, the transfer just isn't there. Whole language theorists understand this. That is why they urge the teaching of skills in the context of whole text. So we recommend teaching skills using the storybook or novel that the students are engaged with at the time. In the primary grades, this is most effectively done using Big Books with the whole group.

POST-READING ACTIVITIES

Following the discussion of the story and the development of skills is the post-reading phase. At this point, an attempt should be made to tie together all the major foci of the book. If the teacher has chosen to highlight character development in the story, then this is an opportunity to allow the students to recapitulate the main character's development through the text. If the plot has been a major emphasis because it has an impact on the main character's growth or deterioration, the questions asked at this point would help the students to trace those events that have caused that change. If predictions had been made at the beginning of the story, their accuracy would be checked in a final review.

It is important to keep in mind that the activity done at this point in the lesson should deal with the entire text and not just the final pages or last chapter. At the middle school level it is acceptable to use this opportunity to ask questions which will check the students comprehension. It is also acceptable to assign questions to the students which require a full written response in a test-like format. It is up to the teacher to decide how formal this should be, but the opportunity to discuss in a final "wrap-up" fashion should not be undervalued. The written copy of the students' responses can be kept on file as a reflection of their comprehension. At the primary level, where the ability to express oneself in written form is still at the developmental stage, this wrap-up would most likely be in the form of a discussion.

LITERATURE EXTENSION ACTIVITIES

We could easily write a volume just on the topic of literature extension activities. What is important to reflect on at this juncture is the purpose for such activities. When we try to move away from a basal program, the structure for teaching in that way will not fade away easily. The notion of seatwork, therefore, may remain firmly in place. There is no question but that a certain portion of children's time in school must be spent in independent activities. There are valuable lessons for them to learn about studying or working on their own. However, the question of the quality of the activities that they do in these contexts must be addressed in a direct way.

When a teacher sits down to plan a literature lesson, thinking should be long range and encompassing rather than fragmented. In other words, decisions must be made ahead of time about what will be highlighted throughout the book. For example, will character be a focus, or setting as it affects the character, or will the events receive major attention because they reveal certain facts about the main character? Sometimes the book is being used to tie into a theme. In that case, the parts of the book that relate to that theme will be the highlight. There is also the possibility that the author will be the main focus if other books by him or her have been read by the class. Whatever the focus is, it should carry throughout the book, not only in the prereading, reading, and post-reading phases, but also into the extension activities.

As the process moves forward during the first couple of years, the role of the library media specialist will change and become even more crucial. She or he will become a resource person for classroom teachers as they start to branch off in a variety of directions. In some cases teachers will need help with finding other titles by a particular author or books having similar themes. For example, a teacher may have used a title from the designated titles list and would like to do an author study. Or the titles used in the classroom may have dealt with friendship or the courage of a young person living in the wilderness. The teacher may wish to use other titles at the same reading level which would expand these ideas. The school librarian is invaluable at this point, recommending and gathering a group of books for the teacher to use in her classroom. This will save classroom teachers a tremendous amount of time they can little afford to spend in this manner. Also, the quality of the selections would be assured.

HELP TEAM MEMBERS DEVELOP THEMES

In addition to this service, the library media specialist's help will also be essential as grade-level members and individual teachers start to develop integrated themes. In about the third year of the process, after classroom teachers have gained some experience with the literature titles and used them with children of all ability levels, the topic of theme development should be introduced. (This is discussed fully in chapter 4.) At that point, continue with the grade-level meeting format. The grade-level team decides on the theme to be developed. First create the *goal* of the theme. This is a very important part of the whole process since everything done with the children relates to this point. For example, a goal for a recycling theme might be:

- Through a variety of experiences with literature, math, science, and social studies students will become aware of the importance that recycling plays in their present life and the future of the world.

Following this step, the teachers develop *objectives* for the theme. These are much more focused statements such as:

- The students will gain an appreciation of the full gamut of the recycling process by visiting the town recycling site and talking with the recycling coordinator.
- The students will expand their letter-writing skills by composing a letter to their state officials encouraging them to consider a state-wide program of recycling.

In the next phase of the theme-development process, the grade-level team will divide the work of developing lessons related to the topic. At this stage, the library media specialist is an essential player. Once the areas of the curriculum which will be integrated into the theme have been decided by the team, each team member will begin to look at the resources which will tie into that content area. In most cases this will lead to the resources of the school library media center and to the librarian. If the library collection is well stocked, the library media specialist will refer the teacher to the specific resources that support a given content area. He or she may also suggest some other sources that may need to be procured from an outside library, and make arrangements to obtain the materials for the teacher. In addition to pointing out various resources, the library media specialist can also be a valuable source in planning the theme, e.g. recommending a direction which the team might not have considered. Whatever the library media specialist's role in this process, there is no question that his or her time, effort, and knowledge can make theme development effective and more likely to achieve its goal.

BUILDING THE COLLECTION

Chapter 5 deals with the library media specialist's role in the purchase of trade books to be used in the literature program. We strongly recommend that trade books be housed in the library media center in a reserved area away from the general collection. The books would be distributed and collected by the library staff under the direction of the librarian. This practice has a number of good points to support it, not the least of which is to ensure that every teacher has the materials needed when they are needed, but also to ensure that the materials will be repaired when necessary or replaced when severely damaged or lost. If the trade books are not cared for in this way, they will deteriorate and will need to be replaced at a much greater rate.

When making decisions about extension activities, it is wise to keep in mind that, as the word denotes, they are intended to *extend* the focus of the literature text. If the teacher has determined ahead of time that the traits of the character will be the focus of a theme tied into social studies or science, then activities should be selected which will further deepen the students' understanding and appreciation of the focus. It is possible to have writing exercises, art activities, cooking activities, presentations or plays, musical performances, field trips, and so on. More specific descriptions of ideas will be given in the next section on workbooks. When you meet to discuss a literature lesson that has been developed by a team member, consider not only the extension activities presented by the teacher who developed the lesson but also those of the other teachers on the team as well as the school librarian. No lesson should be considered complete until after this discussion has taken place. Following this, a completed copy of the entire lesson should be typed and given to team members for their binder.

Finally, remember that the primary focus of the exercise described here is giving the teacher practice in preparing literature lessons. Once that skill has been presented and implemented by teachers, the purpose for continuing it loses value. It should not be continued with the idea that every single book on the designated titles list will have a literature lesson completed. Such a practice would smack of a basal reader manual mentality. Once teachers on a team get a feel for preparing a literature lesson, it is hoped that they will then prepare their own lessons for books. This will promote more creativity and prevent the advance of the deadly stagnation which often cripples enthusiasm for basal reader stories.

WHAT ABOUT WORKBOOKS?

No doubt most of us have read the statistics about the use of workbooks in the classroom. The most commonly cited reference is that in the national study on the state of reading instruction in the United States, *Becoming a Nation of Readers*. In this study we are told that:

> Students spend up to 70% of the time allocated for reading instruction in independent practice or 'seatwork.' This is an hour per day in the average classroom. Most of this time is spent on workbooks and skill sheets. Children spend considerably more time with their workbooks than they do receiving instruction from their teachers (Anderson, et al. 1985, 74).

In addition to this, we have the words of Dolores Durkin in her study of reading comprehension instruction in grades three through six classrooms:

> . . .the overwhelming influence of workbooks and other assignment sheets was unexpected. As was mentioned, it had been taken for granted prior to the study that there would be, in fact should be, some written assignments to provide for practice. But the thought that they

would constitute almost the whole of instructional programs was never entertained. Nonetheless, that was the case (Durkin 1978, 524).

Referring back to our earlier discussion in chapter 1 on the development of the basal reader movement, we must keep in mind the influence of the testing movement on reading instruction. Reading skills, in order to be tested, had to be broken down into discrete units. This, in turn, prompted the teaching of skills in isolation and practice in isolation in order to test in isolation. Enter the reading workbook, the perfect vehicle for practice of skills. Not only could you find a sheet for practice of a skill, in many cases you might have as many as five pages with isolated exercises designed to increase a student's ability to perform. This was the natural transition to the testing phase of the process. In most cases, the student was required to do little more than fill in a blank or circle an answer.

All of us who have worked with children in a basal reading program know only too well that some children are able to function quite well on these isolated practice sheets and yet not comprehend what they read. In addition, there are students who can do the exercises in the workbooks but who do not use the skill in a real-life reading situation when they come upon a word or portion of text that they do not understand. Why does this happen? Whole language theorists believe it happens because the skills are not being taught in the context of natural text. In other words, the students do not see the practice situation as having anything to do with real reading. It is something you do at the end of the story while the teacher is working with the other group. This is commonly referred to as *skill teaching*. What we are striving for in a literature-based reading program is *strategies teaching*. The use of workbooks militates against this.

When you are moving into a literature-based program and you are trying to do it gradually to ensure its growth and development, it is not a good idea to take all their supports out from under the teachers. Therefore, although it is desirable to do away with workbooks eventually, it is best to allow them to be used in tandem with other extension activities that the teachers will create for the first couple of years during the initial implementation phase. Teachers must be given enough time to build up their resources as they move away from the basal. It is our recommendation, therefore, that the workbooks be ordered for any teacher who wants them during the first two years of the program. After that, they should be avoided. Let teachers know that they have some leeway but eventually you will expect them to give over the workbooks in favor of creative, meaningful extension activities.

OTHER OPTIONS FOR SKILLS DEVELOPMENT

How, then, do you help the students to practice the skills they are learning? As was mentioned previously in the section on extension activities, there is a wide variety of options available from which to choose. When the teachers are divorced from the idea of having to use a paper and pencil response, they open up to the possibility of using many options which will be far more appealing to the children and, therefore, perhaps increase their learning. The following suggestions come to us from a book by Terry Johnson and Daphne Louis titled *Literacy Through Literature*. We offer the same caveat in presenting their ideas as we did in offering our suggestions for developing a literature lesson, namely, these should serve as a springboard for other ideas rather than a manual to be followed slavishly. Here are some of their suggestions in nutshell format:

Cloze Variations

1. Burgess Summaries: Provide the students with summaries of a story and delete certain key words replacing them with nonsense words which the students will replace with real words that fit. Another possibility is to delete most of the letters of certain key words and ask the children to complete them. These are good vocabulary building exercises and can also be used to review certain phonics skills.

2. Story Ladders: This extends the cloze procedure by eliminating the second half of a sentence. When using this procedure, a summary of the story is also used. Another variation of this is to focus on one character from the story and to provide the students with sentence stems about the character's appearance or actions in the story which they must complete. Another possibility is to provide a series of stems which summarize the major events in the story. The student would then provide the events.

3. Poetry: Allow the children to explore rhythm and rhyme by deleting rhyming words or other key words from poems the children know.

In each of these cloze exercises the students are seeing the words in context rather than in isolation. Also, a variety of skills can be addressed in each exercise.

Clues:

1. Sight Word Development: To increase understanding of word meanings, try giving students visual clues about a character from a familiar story and have them try to figure out who it is. The focus here is on familiarizing the students with words from the story which they see in a slightly different context.

2. Word Meaning Development: Vary the clues procedure a bit by giving clues that relate to characters in the story on one side of a card and the name of the character or important object on the other. This will involve some inferential thinking.

3. Literary Countdown: A series of clues about a character or object from a story are presented to a class one at a time as the students try to guess the thing being described.

4. Twenty Questions: Students are allowed up to 20 questions about a book, character, or event in an attempt to guess what it is. This could be done orally or in writing.

Illustrations

1. Book Production: Preparing a book for production usually calls for pictures of some sort. This can be done for an individual's book or for a class book. The choices of what to illustrate have to be made by the author(s).

2. Portions of Text: Selecting a portion of the text that has been read and asking the students to illustrate it is a popular practice. The teacher may also discuss what is important for the students to include in the picture.

Story Maps

Johnson and Louis tell us that story maps appear to be a "deceptively simple idea" and the end result "may not look as intellectually demanding nor as pedagogically satisfying as answers to ten comprehension questions" but the creation "demands a very high level of understanding" (Johnson & Louis 1987, 63).

1. Picture story maps: The students are asked to draw pictures to represent major events in the story and then to label them. The events must be presented in a sequential fashion.

2. Written story maps: This type can be done after the picture story map has been presented at the primary level. Essentially, the format used earlier in this chapter on preparing literature lessons is appropriate.

As Johnson and Louis mention, story map making can take many forms and can be as demanding as the teacher desires. For example, the teacher might choose a section of the story that is rife with physical description of the setting and ask the students to draw a story map of that setting including all the relevant features that they have highlighted. They further tell us that the only limitations to map making are "the opportunities presented in the stories encountered, the cartographic skills of the children and your (and their) ingenuity." (Johnson & Louis 1987, 67).

It is important to keep in mind that resources such as the Johnson and Louis book should be used only as a starting point for creating ideas to use in conjunction with skills reinforcement. Be sure they are not permitted to substitute for the teacher's valuable creative energy.

DON'T FORGET WRITING

The "Process Writing Approach," which was introduced by Donald Graves, University of New Hampshire, is an invaluable asset to the development of a literature-based reading program. He theorized that in order to get children to write, we have to prioritize the steps in the process and place more emphasis on helping them to get their ideas down on paper first, show them how to edit their own work. We then focus on the "polishing up" procedure which includes in the final phase attention to grammar, punctuation, spelling, and sentence and paragraph development. The teacher addresses these skills in mini-lessons at the beginning of the writing period and then allows the children to spend time in writing or

---

Other Options for Skill Development

Some other possibilities for skill development are described more fully in Johnson and Louis' book:

- Literary Report Cards (focus on character development)
- Extended Invitations
- Literary Passports
- Literary Posters
- Literary Letters
- Agony Column
- Journals
- Book Awards
- Literary Sociograms
- Literary News Reports
- Plot Profiles
- Literary Interviews
- Structured Writing
- Discussions
- Mime and Drama

conferencing. There is usually a sharing period at the end of each lesson. A fuller description of the approach can be found in Graves' book *Writing: Teachers and Children at Work* (Graves 1983).

Using writing in a literature-based program gives children opportunities to respond to the books they are reading. From first through sixth grade, teachers may use this technique to encourage activities related to the books the children are reading. Some examples are:

Primary Level (K-3):

1. When the children have discussed a sound, have chosen words in a large-format text, and have worked with the teacher to make a list of words containing the sound, the children can choose words from the list to use in a story or poem related to the story from which the original words were drawn.

2. Students can take a repetitive phrase from a book being read and make a book of their own with pictures and captions. For example, following a theme on dinosaurs, the book *If Dinosaurs Were Alive Today* was read aloud to first graders. Following that, the repeated phrase "If dinosaurs were alive today. . ." was chosen and students were asked to make a book of their own offering their own ideas about what it would be like. The books were cut out in the shape of dinosaurs.

3. In grade one, the book *The Very Hungry Caterpillar* is very popular. Following a reading of that book, students could create a book describing the life cycle of a butterfly. This fits in nicely with a science project on this topic.

4. In grade two, following a reading of the story *The Funny Little Woman*, have the children write a story from the dumpling's point of view or rewrite it in the format of a play.

5. In conjunction with the story *Sylvester and the Magic Pebble*, have the students pretend that they are news reporters assigned to write a story about the disappearance of Sylvester.

6. For the book *Blueberries for Sal*, students could be assigned to teams and asked to research the various types of berries found in New England. They would

write about their findings and present a report for the class.

7. In grade three, after reading the book *Molly's Pilgrim*, ask students to interview the members of their families about the arrival of their ancestors in this country. They would create the interview questions, write the responses to them, and prepare a written report for their classmates.

8. In grade three, in the story *My Mother Sends Her Wisdom*, the riddle is presented. The students could be asked to write riddles of their own.

9. Following a reading of *Crow Boy*, the students could be asked to write about their special talents and describe how someone brought out those special talents in some way.

10. In conjunction with the story *Bunnicula, A Rabbit Tale Mystery*, students could be divided into teams each being asked to rewrite any scene in the story from a different point of view. These could be presented to the other students in play format.

Intermediate Level (4-6)

1. In grade four, after reading *The Indian in the Cupboard*, students could be asked to research customs of various Indian tribes who live in the United States and present a report on a comparison of them. They could also be asked to write a story in which they create a diminutive person who is used to get across a message to a group of people. The message could be serious or humorous.

2. Have students at these grade levels focus on the main character in the story and write a description of how he or she changed in some way in the story.

3. At this level, students can be asked to write a comparison of two characters in the story who have dissimilar ways of doing things. They should back up their statements with examples from the text of situations that bear out their characteristics.

4. Timelines are a good writing project and will involve some research. It is a good idea to assign two students to work together in doing the research and creating the timeline which can be done in conjunction with any book that deals with a subject that might have an

historical dimension to it such as sports, inventions, development of a people or a country, or a custom such as dancing or foods.

5. If students are working on historical novels such as *Johnny Tremain*, they can be asked to pick an event in the story that is based on fact and research it for accuracy. Their results can be presented in written form to the class.

6. Students at this level can be asked to explain the relationship of two characters in the story citing examples from the story that reinforce their thoughts.

7. They can be asked if they liked the ending of the story. If they did, they must give examples from the story of the parts that they liked. If they did not, they must explain what they disliked and offer alternative solutions to the ending.

8. At this level it is a good project to take quotations from the text and ask students to react to them in writing. The quotes chosen can relate to character development, description of events that were important to the story, or they can simply be examples of figurative language such as similes or metaphors.

9. If an historical novel is being studied, students can be asked to prepare a debate on a topic related to the historical period during which the novel takes place. Much work in both research and the rudiments of debating would have to be done before an actual encounter would be staged.

10. Comparisons of authors who write in a similar style or about the same period of time is always a good writing project at this level. Also good is a comparison of two characters from two different books who have similar experiences. For example, comparing the main characters in *Maniac Magee* with *The Great Gilly Hopkins* and their experiences would be an interesting writing project.

What cannot be stressed enough in offering these suggestions is that none of them is intended as the be-all and end-all to be used forever. These ideas came from teachers who are trying them daily in their classrooms. It is hoped that these suggestions will lead to new ideas or to adaptations the next time the book is used. In every case, the most important thing to keep in mind is that the creativity of the teacher should be capitalized upon and allowed to flow. If there is no room for that to happen, then the district might as well stay with a basal reading system—with a manual full of set ideas which require little thought and little talent to implement. What will be important is for someone to be available to teachers if they have questions at first about the suitability of a project when used in conjunction with a book. This can be a supervisor, a reading specialist/consultant, the school librarian or a subject area specialist in a building. If these positions do not exist in a school system, it may fall upon either the principal or the grade-level team members to make judgments.

Not only in writing but in any activity related to a literature book, sharing of ideas among professionals who use those books in the classroom will be essential. A positive by-product of this kind of sharing will be the enthusiasm that emanates from the discussions and begins to infuse the reading lessons done with the children. When teachers exude enthusiasm about literature, then children also become excited about it. Eventually children begin to experience the joy of reading. Shouldn't this be our primary focus? If we make learning enjoyable, the children will learn better.

4 ORGANIZING CURRICULUM-ORIENTED PROGRAMS

No other aspect of the literature-based reading program is more important than the reading list on which it is based. It is the embodiment of the philosophy that students will read, enjoy, appreciate, and share quality materials which are complete, not snippets or abridgements. For many students, it is their initiation into the world of literature—books whose writing styles, themes, plots, character development, settings, accuracy, and integrity can stir the imagination and emotions of the reader.

Designing a list which incorporates the philosophical ideals of the program, meets the educational needs of the students, includes a well-balanced selection of many types of literature, and accommodates a range of interest and ability levels for each grade is a challenging task. While there are many quality lists one may examine, no one list should be adopted—even one from another school with the same grade spread and a similar student body or community. Such a list might serve as part of the foundation on which the final list was built as, indeed, would others such as the Newbery and Caldecott award winning and honor books. The crucial point is that the entire faculty must be involved throughout the process of developing the list.

It is vital, also, to keep it a living, growing, and changing list so that there is never a definitive list. This means annual evaluation by the teachers with suggestions for additions and deletions. When a title is dropped from the list it may be considered for reinclusion at another time. Titles often change grade level in order to better fit other curriculum areas or topics. Since each grade level will have students with a wide span of reading levels, there is really no such thing as a "third grade book" or a "fifth grade book." This has always posed great problems in understanding for parents and for teachers new to the profession. Textbook publishers have arbitrarily set levels for what they label third grade or fifth grade but this is a hopeless (and educationally stifling) attempt to create a slot designated as "normal third grader" or "average fifth grader." Further refinements in the publishing world have given rise to 3.5 or 3.9 gradations which are intended to indicate the midpoint or end of the third grade. Still more damaging is the fact that these indicators have been lowered over the past several years to match the decreasing expectations the schools have set for student reading and learning. This "dumbing down" of textbooks has had less of an influence on trade books for young people, but it is there. While established "name" writers can insist on using the vocabulary they feel is necessary for what they are trying to say, authors who have not yet achieved this level of success in the marketplace will either be told to use a less demanding vocabulary or their works will be edited by others to ensure the lower levels. This practice enables publishers to advertise the claim that their books are more readable for today's students. They are also less challenging and less stimulating.

While the purpose of the literature-based reading program is not to reform all of the ills of America's schooling, it can help to hold the line and reverse the trend of watering down content and style until there is little semblance of what makes a book literature and not just another story.

BUILDING THE LIST

To start building a list for any school, choices for inclusion *must* begin with what the library and reading instruction professions have consistently noted as quality materials. To be sure, all experts will not agree on each and every title but a start toward agreement can be made. A good school library media center will have most, if not all, of these titles. Any titles not in the collection should be purchased immediately and/or borrowed from another library. Despite the success of catalog mail order businesses, most people need to see the real article, not just hear or read about it. Since the only titles that will be in consideration are those that are available in paperback, the investment in single copies of titles for perusal is not very large. Out of this number many will be chosen and, since all were recommendations from quality listings, the remainder will be fine additions to the library media center collection. Representatives of each of the grade levels should be meeting at regular intervals and, between meetings, should be reading the titles in consideration and reporting back to their grade teams as well as the selection group. There needs to be much give-and-take because the final product will be a grid of titles which cover the interest and ability variables of the students at every grade level. Also taken into account will be many genres, from biography to science fiction, and those works which integrate well with other aspects of the curriculum such as American history for fifth grade social studies or animal habitats for first grade science.

TEACHER CONCERNS

Teachers will have many concerns during this process and they must all be addressed—both those that are stated and those that lie just below the surface and are not articulated. One decision which should be agreed upon at the outset is that no teacher (or substitute) may read aloud to a class a book which is a designated title for a higher grade. There may be some dispute about this as teachers have their favorite books which they dearly love to share with their students. However, there is no dearth of wonderful materials to read aloud to awaken a love of good books. What is at risk, however, is the ability of a teacher, in the grade to which that title was allocated, to use techniques such as prediction of plot development or character change with the students. Swearing to secrecy the three students out of a class of 25 who know the ending of a mystery story is futile. It may be argued that some pupils will have read certain titles. True, and some will have seen an animated film version of the story. But a teacher reading aloud to a whole class, with understandably natural discussion occurring, is a different matter.

At the lower end of the grid for any grade level will be titles that could just as easily have been placed at the upper end of the previous grade. Similarly, at the upper end of the grid for any grade level will be materials that could have been assigned to the lower level of the following grade. While it is clearly understood that no teacher may encroach on the materials for a higher grade, it can also be agreed that a teacher may use materials from a lower grade level provided that they are not needed by that grade level at the same time and that they may be recalled for that grade level's use. When these conditions are agreed to at an early stage in the planning, most teachers' minds will be put at ease. It is also imperative that there be sufficient materials at both ends of the grid at each grade level to make compliance comfortable.

There will be, of course, vested interests in certain titles. Statements such as ". . .but we've always done Susan Cooper" or "fifth graders won't understand *My Brother Sam is Dead*" need to be recognized as the quibbles that they are. Most objections dissolve with the promise that there will be enough materials to guarantee the success of the program. The importance of this aspect cannot be overemphasized. In these days of severe budget cuts no part of the curriculum may be guaranteed security. However, an administration that believes in a literature-based reading program must be willing to make other sacrifices to guarantee that the numbers of titles and copies of books necessary to ensure the developing stages of the program will not be curtailed. Career teachers have a long and bitter memory of programs, innovative techniques, and new methodologies that were instituted with the promise of the materials required to put them into practice. The materials were not purchased and, inevitably, even the most gung-ho enthusiasts could no longer make the program work.

Literature-based reading programs in which teachers are asked in September to submit a list of titles they want and the approximate dates they need them are doomed to fail. This is not the way to promote creative teaching. No teacher can successfully anticipate and match student needs and interests ten months in advance. Even with a newly adopted curriculum (and recency of adoption is no reason for every area to remain static) at the start of the school year, each class is a constantly growing and maturing group with unknown and untried potential. While this is true for all age and grade levels, it is especially so in the primary grades.

A necessary building block for the program is the coalition of the library media specialists and the reading teachers as devout believers in and supporters of the literature-based approach. Their enthusiasm alone won't ensure success but the lack of it will guarantee difficulties, if not disaster. Perhaps the motivating force behind the move toward a literature-based reading program was that of a pair of fourth-grade classroom teachers, the building-level director of curriculum, or the system-wide reading consultant. Whatever the original impetus, a majority of the staff involved must reach the critical mass necessary for a successful program.

MANAGING THE MATERIALS

The nuts and bolts management of the materials for the literature-based reading program should emanate from the library media center. Its staff has the experience and expertise in purchasing, processing, mending, circulating, tracking, and record keeping necessary for the efficient management of such an operation. This is not a question of turf. It is a school-wide program for which materials need to be housed and distributed with dispatch and accuracy. If the library media program does not operate in this manner *before* the installation of the literature-based reading program, the solution is to clean up its act, *not* to try to work around it with makeshift arrangements operating out of the principal's closet, the custodian's supply room, or shelves in the reading teacher's office. These folks have full schedules that do not lend themselves to the tasks previously mentioned. Library media teachers are trained to be resource specialists with extensive knowledge of nontext materials. In the formulation of the reading list they need to take a leadership role. They should be contributing suggestions for titles, making established lists available to the faculty, and giving many booktalks to both small groups of teachers and individuals who are concerned with the construction and quality of the list. They are also aware of any conflict of titles with other programs, such as reading incentive programs that exist at the local or system level or those of the public library. Their knowledge of the entire school curriculum is particularly valuable in selecting materials which can do double or triple duty by serving the reading curriculum and also assisting a topical or interdisciplinary approach to teaching other areas.

Because of the textbook tradition in which many teachers and administrators were raised, thinking about the numbers of copies needed for the operation of the program may tend to follow the reasoning that a few excellent titles with plenty of copies of each is the direction in which the program should go. This is a short-sighted and stifling plan, the logical progression of which is to put all these materials in each classroom. This is an unwarranted expense for materials which will sit idle most of the year. What is worse is that it narrows rather than broadens the literature experiences of the students, negating a major rationale for the program. Choice has been found to be an important motivating factor in many aspects of education. Enthusiasm is generated when both students and teachers have the option to sample a variety of materials from an extensive rather than proscriptive list. A larger list with fewer copies of each title allows for a multiplicity of uses that a slimmer list with great numbers of copies never could.

BEWARE OF THE QUICK FIX

If there is a promising new direction in education could industry be far behind? Of course not. The commercial world has clasped "whole language" with a vengeance and has invested a lot of money in it. At the last annual meeting of the International Reading Association more than half the exhibits were touting either materials proclaimed by their publishers as whole language materials or promoting a "complete whole language program." The latter type is the most seductive and the most dangerous of all. No single publisher's stock of titles can equal a choice made from all the offerings of the multitude of good publishers. No publisher can offer the range of materials necessary to support what is educationally sound and desirable. No commercial enterprise knows your students, teachers, and curriculum. What is offered is a quick fix for big bucks with big appeal: for classroom teachers who can envision the numbers of hours serving on the list selection committees will take; for the impatient consultants who want to put a program into operation before any more years go by; for ambitious administrators who have knowledgeable parents snapping at their heels and Board of Education members asking why it takes so long to put a plan into practice. But, like so many other good ideas superimposed without at least a majority of the faculty's understanding and acceptance, it will lack the enthusiasm necessary for adoption and *use* which is the crux of the matter. Teachers who did not buy into the program may not oppose it in open discussion, speak up at grade level team meetings, or make negative remarks at a small table in the lunchroom. But when they close their classroom doors their attitudes can cripple, if not destroy, what the program should do for students. This is the ultimate waste of the taxpayers' money. Time taken, effort made, and money spent, to help teachers develop their own rationales and eventually win their support is not only educationally sound, beneficial for the students, and a worthwhile contribution to the building of a happy school, it is also cost efficient.

THE INTERDISCIPLINARY APPROACH

The terms *integrated* and *interdisciplinary*, as well as the phrase *across the curriculum*, are perhaps as misunderstood, misinterpreted, and misused as the term whole language itself. What they all refer to, however, is the logical extension of what whole language aims to do in making the written and spoken word meaningful in the life, experience and learning of the child. Educational research, teacher experience, and common-sense observation of student behaviors show clearly that relating what is already known to new information is effective. Also, there is widespread agreement that there is a range of learning styles, backgrounds and interests among all segments of the student population, regardless of age levels.

We have seen that reading textbooks or basals may inhibit or, at worst, curtail reading and writing proficiency by breaking up new information into meaningless pieces in a stultifying progression which takes into account neither the diversity of students' interests, abilities, and experiences nor the myriad topics they will be encountering in other school subjects. The social studies and science textbooks suffer from the same myopia and are even more sensitive to the realities of acceptance by the marketplace. Thus, while it may not have been the goal, the end result is that new editions of these textbooks may have less controversial content, addressing children with little respect for what they know, are interested in, or are capable of learning.

Educators and/or people who work with children have known for many years that reinforcement, not repetition, is what leads to lasting knowledge. Some individuals can see that when a child has proved able to do long division on ten examples, there is nothing to be gained from doing 20 more. Yet these supposedly enlightened people will use the "more of the same" methodology by having students who finish a textbook of one series by Publisher X go to the *same level* in another series by Publisher Y. The infuriating justification is that the children can't go ahead because "what will they do next year?" The missing and hardly-ever-mentioned ingredient is student motivation, the most powerful incentive a teacher can use. What then is the difference between these boring, incentive-killing tactics and reinforcement? Showing, or better yet, letting students discover the relationships between old and new learning underlies the new concepts and exhibits linkages in many areas.

If using the literature itself—entire books written by good authors and not abridged for reading levels—is more meaningful and enjoyable for children does it not follow that history, geography, and all of the sciences should also be offered the same way? The textbook prescribes the curriculum, narrows children's exposure, and helps mainly the teacher who uses the Teacher's Edition for lesson plans. With no textbooks, but with *resource-based learning*, gearing the curriculum to the abilities, interests, and needs of the individual child becomes a reality. This requires many books on the same topic which can serve a wide array of students. It also means a collection as varied as the multitudinous topics covered by the curriculum in all grades of the school. Economy, if not good sense, indicates the need for a school library media center where this vast multifaceted collection of materials in many formats can be organized efficiently, cared for, and loaned to each classroom.

No cost comparisons have been done and a meaningful analysis acknowledging the many variables would be extremely difficult. However, if the fifth grade studies the explorers and early settlers of America in September and October shouldn't those materials on the Plymouth colonists be available to other classes wanting materials on Thanksgiving in November? When the first graders study animals in science and the second graders need materials on various land masses with their indigenous flora and fauna for social studies shouldn't the materials be shared? This is not just better use of the tax dollars. It allows for the needed range of coverage and an opportunity for children to learn how some books and/or authors meet their needs better than others. One book may have better maps, another splendid illustrations, still another may have the definitive index.

The interdisciplinary approach to teaching/learning takes into account all of these matters we have discussed and does so in a way that is challenging and exciting for both the teacher and the learner. There is no Teacher's Edition and no tests provided by the same publisher that created the text. The entire curriculum is covered, but in creative topic-oriented themes. Most, if not all, of the subject areas: language arts, science, mathematics, social studies, art, music, physical education, and even foreign language may be involved. In schools where a grade teacher is responsible for several of these curriculum areas it is natural to carry the theme "across the curriculum" but in schools where there are, for example, art, music, and gym teachers, these specialists need to be consulted and planned with to bring about an integrated program. Some schools have taken on a theme for the year per grade. A few have tried a theme for the whole school for a period of time extending from a week (Western Massachusetts) to a year (Florida) but this can become tedious and defeat the purpose. Topics fall naturally within school curricula and making the connections runs the gamut from easy for some teachers to laborious for others, and all the gradations between.

Brainstorming sessions with grade-level teacher teams, either in the same school if it is large enough or among schools if it is not, is an effective way to hasten the adoption of the integrated curriculum. Several examples need to be prepared to model and then the creative juices should be allowed to flow. Each idea should be written on a card and those judged best shared with the group. All cards should be saved since ideas not immediately useful might have merit at a future time.

A FIFTH GRADE EXAMPLE

The fifth grade social studies curriculum is American history in most schools of the nation. In one school the list of the literature-based reading program for that grade contains 32 titles including many genres. Among the titles in historical fiction are: *Witch of Blackbird Pond* (colonial America); *My Brother Sam is Dead*, *Johnny Tremain*, and *Sarah Bishop* (Revolutionary War); *Slave Dancer*, *Island of the Blue Dolphins*, *The Adventures of Tom Sawyer*, and *April Morning* (19th century); *Sounder*, *The Summer of My German Soldier* and *The Upstairs Room* (first half of the 20th century); and several titles of modern realistic fiction to represent the latter half of this century. Obviously, if the students are reading these titles for language arts they are reinforcing their understanding of the periods in America's history with which the books deal. In addition, every child is required to read a book about people and events in each of the four centuries: 17th through 20th. The types of reporting on these last four required readings vary widely. To start the year there is also another requirement of reading a book on "Discoverers" which may be fiction or nonfiction about an astronaut, a science pioneer, a surgeon, an inventor, etc., or the more prosaic Marco Polo, Christopher Columbus, or Magellan. Map skills and geography lessons are are done with each selection.

Timelines are worked out by each student throughout the year by means of a computer program.

The library media center stocks 25 copies of each of the literature-based reading titles. For the "Discoverers" assignment or each of the "Century" assignments, the library media staff pulls 150 to 200 books (125 to 175 titles) since the "slow grabbers" need to find plenty of books to choose from so they don't feel they were offered less choice than the "eager beavers" had. There are approximately 100 students in the five classes of the school's fifth grade. Following the assignment the students are scheduled into the library media center in two successive waves of 50. They find all the books face-up on six tables—very much like the book fairs with which the children are familiar. The library media specialist walks around the tables with the students answering questions and giving quickie booktalks. All students must have their teachers' approval of their choices so that better readers are challenged and poorer readers can find sufficient appropriate materials. Special Education students may be offered materials previously selected for their needs by the library media specialist in cooperation with the teachers, but they should participate in the book fair selection process with their classmates. The books for these assignments are charged out to the individual students with the right to renew until the assignment is completed. No fines are charged anyway, but the normal loan period is two weeks. This suits a few students, but most renew at least once.

A FIRST GRADE EXAMPLE

In one New England school the first graders all study "Seasons" as both science and social studies curriculum. Since the region is famous for its fall foliage display, much is done with leaves in the classroom including mathematics papers in simple addition. The art teachers pursue the theme with reference to shapes, colors, and sizes of the leaves, and of the trees both with and without their foliage. Easy Fiction and Easy Nonfiction books circulate to the classrooms on autumn, seasonal changes, animals getting ready for the approaching winter, trees, leaves, apples, climate and its influence on people, plants, and animals. Much is done with poetry in the fall and again in the spring. In late September all first graders have a field trip to a large local orchard where they may pick apples and watch a cider press in operation. The physical education teachers and the music teachers also use the seasons/leaves/apples themes in their classes.

The theme or topic approach is old hat to kindergarten and first grade teachers. Weaving themes together with the literature-based reading program presented a new challenge. With the publication of paperback nonfiction books for the beginning reader it became easier to combine what the reading groups were reading with the topic. Many of these materials were originally from Australia or New Zealand but they are now available from several publishers in the United States.

A FOURTH GRADE EXAMPLE

A typical school's fourth grade social studies curriculum is concerned with the origins of the people who came to what is now the United States. They start with Native Americans and the literature-based reading program titles are: *The Sign of the Beaver, Indian in the Cupboard*, and *Return of the Indian* (showing the stereotypical views of English schoolboys). Information on the local Native American tribes (those still in existence as well as those that are gone) is the start and then each student chooses another tribe from some other region. Comparisons and contrasts are made between the two tribes as to clothing, food, transport, housing, customs, etc. These assignments call for a great deal of time in the library media center. All pertinent materials are pulled and placed on book trucks. Classes sign up in advance to come in singly or in pairs with their teachers. At first, half-hour blocks are sufficient, but later the students can handle 45-minute or even full hour sessions effectively. The reports, hand-made artifacts (hatchets, spears, canoes), layouts of Indian villages, and so on, that result from this study are remarkable. There is a field trip to an Indian Museum and a wigwam the students put together is right outside the fourth grade wing. The music and physical education teachers really enjoy this theme. Last year the Art teacher had all the fourth graders make storyteller dolls out of clay or papier-mâché. The library media specialist had brought in her small storyteller doll as an example and had several books and articles showing many types of dolls. There are no Native American children in this school. Two years ago the Parent Teacher Organization brought in a Native American storyteller and poet who not only entertained but encouraged the students in their poetry writing.

Following this ethnic group come studies of Africans, the slave trade, and modern African Americans. The literature-based reading books are: *Journey to Jo'burg, The Hundred Penny Box, Frederick Douglass Fights for Freedom, Zeely,* and *Freedom Train: the Story of Harriet Tubman.* Other titles in the program which deal with ethnicity are: *The Night Journey* (Jews in Russia), *Today's Special Z.A.P. and Zoe* (Greek Americans), *In the Year of the Boar and Jackie Robinson* (Chinese Americans), and *Wheel on the School* (Netherlands.) The students trace their own ancestry and the routes taken by various people who came to America. Their map skills, geography lessons, and math skills are used to plot these routes and estimate time spent and modes of transportation used. Then each student becomes a "travel agent" and plans a trip around the world choosing various places to visit and must coordinate the transportation and the costs (and the exchange rates in each country). This is a lengthy process making great use of almanacs and atlases.

Even from these sketchy outlines it is easy to see what excitement can be generated from resource-based teaching/learning. The titles in the literature-based reading program were chosen by the teachers and the library media specialist because they are excellent books that also dovetailed with the curriculum. Some titles were added in the second year of the program and some were transferred from other grade levels. In the first year of the program the sixth grade wanted *Witch of Blackbird Pond* but a case for the fifth grade curriculum was made and so another title was traded.

The sixth grade teachers are currently caught up in the interdisciplinary approach and intend to add titles of high quality which deal with India, Japan, China, the Middle East, and the many nations that were once the Soviet Union. They are enjoying the search which means that when new titles are found the enthusiasm level for the teaching will be very high.

WORKING WITH TEACHERS

It seems obvious that reading teachers could have no greater helpmates, nor stronger supporters for their programs than library media specialists. However, the close sense of partnership that should exist is not always present. Each profession has a complementary role in the development of readers.

While reading teachers are concerned with making sure that students have mastered the skills and techniques necessary for reading, they are also intent upon having students become competent, confident lovers of reading. Library media specialists are less involved with the teaching of many of the basic reading skills. They are concerned with the reinforcement of others (mainly in the comprehension category) and focus on creating readers, information retrievers, and lifetime learners. They want to make sure not only that children can read but that they do read. Those of us who drive know full well that we really became drivers *after* we got our licenses and had been driving for a while. We not only knew how to drive, we were drivers with all the sharpened instinctual knowledge born of familiarity and would be such all of our lives. In the same way those who have learned to read only become *readers* with lots of enjoyable practice.

As partners in the process of turning students into lifetime learners, the reading teachers and library media specialists work hand-in-hand. This is particularly easy to achieve with the literature-based reading program. They need to pool their knowledge of reading levels, children's tastes and preferences, classroom teachers' proclivities and teaching styles, and the vast and wonderful world of books. This partnership is a tremendous boon for the classroom teacher and eliminates duplicated efforts, redundancy, and wasteful spending of the ever-shrinking public funds. Reading teachers today are dealing with larger percentages of the student population identified as needing special assistance. This is partly because state testing is focusing more narrowly on reading problems of all sorts. It is also because the years of "dumbing down" the textbooks, and many of the trade books as well, have taken their toll.

Children's reading habits have undergone great change in the past half century most of which are a direct result of television in their lives. They are used to receiving information faster and more superficially than the pace of a well-written book would give them. Just as television dramas hook viewers with the story before they can turn the dial or hit the zapper (and then roll the opening credits and commercials) so do junior novels get well into the plot in the first page and a half. Descriptions of setting, circumstances and the like are kept to a minimum and much plot and character development is done through dialog. Children exposed to the whistles and bells of *Sesame Street* and the catchy appeal of commercials do not always settle down happily with the kinds of books their parents enjoyed in their childhood.

Fortunately, there are thousands of children's books published each year for all tastes: weapons to warlocks, knights to kittens, spiders to spaceships. The quality of the paper, the printing, and especially the illustrations, have never been better. Unfortunately, the prices of hardbound books have skyrocketed, but there are more paperbacks available than ever before. One of the most important improvements has been the increased number of high-quality nonfiction books for the prereading and beginning reading child. Many children will eagerly borrow nonfiction books with color photographs on subjects in which they are interested and struggle to read the text but will not even borrow, much less open and try to read books which are "not real." Sadly, some well-meaning teachers and library media specialists who are themselves picture book aficionados do not understand these children's preferences and deem them uninterested in books and reading. They are only uninterested in reading those books, not all books.

In addition to knowing books and other materials, library media specialists must excel in their knowledge of curriculum. They have to know many facets of every discipline, what is taught at every grade level, and at what time of the year. It is imperative that they anticipate the needs of the teachers, not merely fulfill requests. Clerks can respond to requests for materials. Professionals must not only order to support the curriculum and the diverse learning styles of the children, but continuously offer new materials and solicit suggestions from the entire staff. Somehow the library media specialists must arrange to meet with teachers at team levels, in small groups, and individually. They must also visit classrooms or, at least, look in to see the latest displays of the children's work or decorations. This interest is much appreciated by the children and the teachers and it keeps the library media specialists informed about the nuances of the teaching approaches and methodologies. Delivering a set of the literature-based reading books affords just such an opportunity. If the grade teachers all have their preparation time scheduled in the same timeslot it makes meeting with them as a grade level team much easier, but one way or another the dialog will take place if the intent is there.

Some administrations may assume that the literature-based reading program is the exclusive domain of the reading teachers. This is very short-sighted at best and impractical at worst. Reading teachers have enough to do without ordering, processing, mending, distributing, collecting, and inventorying books. These are skills that library media specialists practice on a daily basis. Space for storing these materials all together is another major consideration. To believe that a grade teacher is going to have every class every year read the same titles at the same time is to ignore the individuality of each class and the stimulation a teacher gets from new approaches and/or variations. Very often the grade teacher will simply browse the storage shelves, which is far more inspiring and helpful to decision making than simply perusing the printed list of titles for the grade. Even after four or five years teachers may ask the library media specialist for suggestions about which titles would make a more meaningful sequence for special youngsters or groups of readers. This is how titles to read aloud, that are good companions, and enhancers to the designated titles in the literature-based reading program, are suggested to the teachers by an alert librarian.

A strong collection of alphabet books is, of course, of great importance for the preschool, kindergarten, and first grade children. They are also of tremendous value to fifth graders in fostering their creative writing skills, teaching search skills, organization techniques, layout and design principles, and respect for the work that goes into the making of a "simple" book.

Stories without words, a genre of books usually considered material only for the not-yet-reading child, are excellent means for getting students to give their interpretations and then make comparisons. Easy picture dictionaries are invaluable for not only ESL students of all ages but also for those studying foreign language to use as vocabulary drills or self-tests.

Adventure books or survival stories lend themselves to discussion about how one might cope under various conditions, such as a different climate, another time period, or another part of the world. The library media specialist needs to be able to provide suggested titles for comparisons. Biographies of people who lived at a particular time or in a given place may convey a better, more rounded picture than an encyclopedia article which has the facts but does not breathe life into them. This form of narrative history or the historical novel which tells you how the people felt about things provides for more true understanding and learning than mere lists of what people ate, wore, and made, whether in ancient Greece or colonial America. Again, other books which treat the same period, country, state, and/or conditions should be offered for contrast.

In short, library media specialists should be such an integral part of what goes on in the classroom that teachers and students cannot imagine it any other way.

COOPERATING FOR SUCCESS

Successful teaching/learning is greatly enhanced when the library media specialist and grade or special teacher plan cooperatively. Most library media specialists and teachers make this part of their efforts when there is new curriculum to be explored or when there is a desire to try new approaches or units in the customary curriculum. Truly creative teachers will use this partnership for even tried and proven lesson plans that have worked well in previous years. When there are sufficient titles in the literature-based reading program the classroom teacher can match the needs of the reading group or class at that month, season, semester, or year.

Currently, ethnic diversity is a major thrust in education and there is a multitude of titles among prize-winning novels and runners-up from which good selections can be made. Thematic units whether independent of or integrated with the science and/or social studies curriculum areas are natural and common approaches. Thus, *Frederick Douglass Fights for Freedom*, *The Hundred Penny Box*, *Zeely*, *Journey to Jo'burg*, and *Freedom Train* in the fourth grade list will more likely be used during February, which is Black History Month, but any of those titles can be combined in regional area studies or in a discussion of stereotypes and misinterpretations.

Some occurrences are serendipitous and the interest that is generated from one of the books in the literature-based reading program can be carried through to new exciting areas spurred on by the students' curiosity or desire to learn more about a topic. For example: a class reading *King of the Wind* was unacquainted with the term "mute" which described the main character who was groom and trainer of the Arabian stallion of the title. This naturally led to discussions of blindness and deafness and the classic example of a person who overcame that duplicate handicap, Helen Keller. Biographies of Keller and her remarkable teacher Anne Sullivan Macy were then explored as well as those of Louis Braille. One of the students talked of a kindergartner who rode on her school bus who was adept at signing and soon all the books on sign language were taken as well. Most of the youngsters were quite familiar with signing since a local television station routinely had a person signing in a corner of the screen during the morning and evening news broadcasts. But knowing that one of their own student body, and a kindergartner at that, could sign was a real incentive to become better acquainted with the alphabet and to try their hands at it.

In one school the fourth grade social studies curriculum deals with immigration and the ethnic roots of Americans. The reading list includes 14 related titles as well as hundreds of folktales cataloged and labeled by country of origin to make it easy for both students and teachers to locate tales for the country they have chosen to investigate in greater depth. This is also done for books which deal with celebrations of specific peoples. The science curriculum for that grade deals with land masses and so the collection of materials on individual countries is extremely large and is in fairly continuous use.

USING THEMATIC APPROACHES

There are a number of books on the market which deal with using a thematic approach to the teaching of reading through literature, and the library media center should stock many of them in the professional collection. Some of these books contain a great variety of lesson plans, models of artwork, sample forms, bookmark suggestions, etc. which are geared to several grade levels. They are formatted to facilitate duplication and even the most independent and creative teachers love to flip through these books for ideas.

A natural outgrowth of literature-based programs is that children who have particularly enjoyed a book come in small groups to the library media center to investigate other books by the same author or similar books by other authors. *Aldo Applesauce* may lead to the modern realistic fiction of Patricia Reilly Giff or Suzy Kline. This is a golden opportunity for the library media specialist to do a booktalk on books in series for the whole class or even the whole grade. The offer of a booktalk is always well received but most teachers will hesitate to ask and so the offer has to be made regularly. Sometimes a book may have a sequel which a percentage of the children will ask to read, for example, *The Bears' House*. Other titles may also have a prequel or companion title such as the works of Cynthia

Voigt. It is imperative that library media specialists keep teachers apprised of these "connections" as well as of the publication of new books by popular authors.

Sometimes an individual teacher or a grade team will request help with a specific problem or outline a desired activity or outcome. For example, one first grade team wished to enhance the reading/writing aspects of the language arts program by having very short stories or poems on laminated sheets so the children could react to and/or illustrate them on computers. The library specialist recognized the tie-in with the science curriculum on animals and suggested fables by Aesop. Fables are, by definition, short and have animal characters. The vocabulary poses problems, however, so the media specialist took 15 fables and rewrote them to meet the reading needs (allowable since Aesop is in the public domain). The specialist then consulted with the teachers about which computer programs have suitable graphics to accomplish the desired results. Short verse at the appropriate levels was much easier to find and credit was assigned for each known poet.

At the second grade level *Doctor De Soto* and *Albert's Toothache* are both on the reading list so there is a logical tie-in with both National Dental Care Month and the health curriculum. But an even more interesting unit is the one that was developed on careers (of the students' relatives, friends, and neighbors) which lasts for about a month. A surprising number of the books on the literature-based reading list matched that unit and the library media specialist adds continuously to the easy nonfiction titles which serve the unit. A more difficult task was to go through all of the fiction and add subject headings which identified jobs and professions of main characters. This effort was taken in stages starting with the specific careers the teachers identified as being common to the lists made by the children. While this is indeed a formidable task, the library media specialist was pleased to gain the better insight into the fiction collection which this specific need brought about.

One of the most exciting occurrences in teaching is brainstorming ideas related to the curriculum. Unfortunately, the opportunities appear to present themselves infrequently, but it is important to be alert to them or even to create them. When administrators see the value of this methodology and allow, or better yet, encourage it by setting aside time in staff meetings or inservice programs for such creative activities, the enthusiasm, new ideas, untried approaches which result are a boost to the morale of the faculty and invigorate the students as well.

PROGRAM EXTENSION

A CASE STUDY

There are a multitude of ways in which the literature-based reading program provides the opportunities to make small segues or quantum leaps into other areas of the curriculum. For example, in one school the initial dedicated list for the second grade contained eight prize-winning titles all of which were folklore of Native Americans and nations such as France, Russia, China, Japan, and Vietnam. The scope of the social studies curriculum is global in grades two, four, and six. Grades one, three, and five concentrate on the western hemisphere. Within a month after school opening all the second graders begin doing "projects" which call for extensive use of the library media center for information on other countries of the world and their people. Twice a week two sixth grade classes work one-on-one with second graders. The inspiration for the younger children is as tremendous as their awe for the "big kids" but an equal benefit is the reinforcement of search techniques for the older students proving once again that real learning comes about through teaching. Geography, especially map skills, is an important part of this unit and there is extensive use of atlases and beginning use of almanacs.

On the fourth grade literature-based reading list there are novels dealing with other cultures, places, and time periods. A natural tie-in during the pre-Hanukkah/Christmas/Kwanzaa weeks is the study of celebrations of all kinds in other lands and other cultures, both in the present and in earlier times. The library media specialist does an introduction to the required search for a legend or fairy tale from the student's chosen country or culture. After an explanation about why these authentic folktales are in the 300s of the nonfiction section and how the books are labeled (398.2 plus the country of origin in capital letters, e.g. 398.2 FRANCE) the students set out eagerly to find a tale. It is the fondest hope of the library media specialist that next year each student's report will include telling the story rather than paraphrasing it in writing. This is a school where the library media specialist tells (not reads) a story each week to every kindergarten and first grade child.

Throughout most of the country fifth grade social studies is concerned with United States history rather than with American history. Both start out the same way through the exploration and colonial periods but after the Revolutionary War studies the rest of the year is spent concentrating on the growth from the original 13 colonies to the 50 states. The literature-based reading program and a western hemisphere focus allow for simultaneous coverage of neighboring Canada and Mexico as well as Central and South America. Large wall maps in both the Spanish and French languages showing the entire hemisphere are excellent tools for tying geography and history together. Students are better able to comprehend why certain rivers, cities, and states have the names that they do when they can see where the Native American tribes were, where the French, English, and Spanish explored, settled, and built fortifications, and how the names were spelled, pronounced, and perhaps changed.

Poetry and songs are important segments of these studies as are crafts and model building. An "Art-Goes-to-School" enrichment program done by volunteers in the community focuses directly on art of the Americas by artists of the western hemisphere depicting scenes from its history. Sets of slides and transparencies are housed in the library and are loaned to the volunteer docents for their edification and/or use in the classrooms. Another emphasis is on architecture, an area of interest previously only lightly touched upon. New materials have been added to the library media collection and contacts have been made with local architects. Wonderful posters were obtained from professional national architecture associations whose members have a genuine interest in seeing more about architecture included in public school curricula.

Sometimes the content flow of the curriculum topics goes in the other direction. For example, when the sixth grade science curriculum is astronomy the library media collection is well-stocked with materials on the planets, comets, asteroids, and so on. There are also many maps and charts of the constellations for the stargazers who will come in at least once during a clear cold spell in the winter to look through the school telescope at 5 a.m. when it is still quite dark. In addition, there is a fine collection of Greek and Roman myths which is a natural outgrowth of studying the constellations and other heavenly bodies. That, in turn, leads to Norse mythology or to a comparison between myths and legends. Not to be overlooked is the wealth of poetry and art with classical mythological themes.

The second grade science curriculum concerns itself with land masses (arctic lands, deserts, seashores, etc.) and so the literature-based reading program has included titles which cover those topographical areas and their flora and fauna. The library media collection must then have large amounts of materials that add to those studies including individual books on the specific animals, birds, insects, or plants that the students will need.

The first grade science curriculum includes spiders, frogs and toads, and butterflies. These subjects will be found in the literature-based reading program titles, both fiction and nonfiction as well. Where possible, Big Books which treat these topics are purchased, too, with sets of ten Little Books to go with each. The Big Book and Little Books sets are purchased and processed by the library media center staff and hung in hang-up bags in storage closets in the respective grade level areas of the school (kindergarten and first grade) where the teachers have ready access to them. They are hung on rods which have replaced the shelves of standard three-foot bookcases.

5 ACQUISITION AND PROCESSING OF THE COLLECTION

ACQUISITION

CHOOSING A PAPERBACK SUPPLIER

When all the appropriate parties have decided on the list of titles for each grade, and ascertained that each selected title is in print and available in paperback, the ordering procedure begins. The library media staff, whose regular duties include the ordering of nontextbook materials for the school, would order from their usual sources which give the maximum discount for paperbacks. Since the titles for the literature-based reading program were chosen on the basis of their literary merit and not from publishers' or other suppliers' catalogs, the publishers of the selected paperbacks would be numerous. The most economical way for schools to order is through book jobbers who maintain large inventories of paperbacks from all the major publishers and give substantial discounts. The amount of discount offered is on the basis of yearly purchasing, so cooperative arrangement plans with other systems or by county or state are the most beneficial and allow the smallest schools to enjoy the same discount as the largest systems. In Connecticut, for example, there are six Cooperating Library Service Units (CLSU) covering the entire state. These independent, incorporated organizations offer some services unique to their areas and other services on a statewide cooperative basis. Among the latter are purchasing agreements with the largest providers of books, videos, school and library supplies, etc. The savings realized on a single book order may be greater than the annual dues charged for membership in the local CLSU. Annual membership in the CLSU provides for the yearly purchasing discount rights with each of the suppliers and all ordering, billing, and payment arrangements may be made on an individual school or school system basis.

THE TIME FACTOR

Small paperback distributors who may offer you a reasonable discount will have to take your order and send it off to each of the publishers on your list. By the time they receive the materials, repack, and ship them to you many precious months may have elapsed. Even the largest book jobbers may not have all your requests in stock. They will ship what they have and then back-order the rest. Because of their size they are continuously being restocked by the publishers and they promise the balance in 60 days. Delays in getting orders out to the supplier must be avoided. Batching of orders leads to these delays as well as increased likelihood of clerical error due to the size and complexity of the task.

SHIPPING CHARGES

Another important consideration in choosing the paperback supplier is the matter of whether the supplier or the recipient will pay the shipping costs. If truckers, UPS, or the postal system is used, shipping costs may represent a substantial percentage of the cost.

ORDERING

Purchase orders should be sent piecemeal by grade level rather than one large all-grade order—for several reasons:

- Each grade level order would have a unique purchase order number, date of order, and date of receipt.
- Stepped or staggered ordering puts less burden on clerical personnel, permitting them to continue their other tasks.
- Lengthy lists are subject to increased clerical errors especially in the case of ISBN numbers (International Standard Book Numbers are the ten-digit number codes which represent publisher, title, editions, etc., and are the means by which orders are filled and billed).
- Shipments of these orders would also be staggered and easier to accession, check for accuracy and/or omission,

and follow through with the supplier for rectification or adjustment.
- Subsequent processing routines can be graduated so they do not become an overwhelming chore.

PROCESSING CHOICES

Books may be ordered from the large book jobbers as single titles or in whatever multiples you may need. In addition to the books themselves, you have the option, for a fee, to have the books sent processed, with kits, or with catalog card sets only. You can also have them added to your inventory database. There are pros and cons for each:

Processed: The books will arrive with labels affixed to the spine and transaction cards and pockets will be pasted in either the front or back according to your stated preference. The catalog card set for each book will be included or inserted in the pocket. As to what is printed on the label, the card, and the pocket, there is very limited choice for the set fee. Specialized processing may carry a hefty price. Neither customary nor specialized processing will provide the laminating or hinging which will lengthen the useful life of the paperbacks and also make them so much more attractive and appealing to the students. We will discuss this point later on in discussions of in-house processing.

Kits: These are packets made up of labels, a transaction card and pocket, and catalog card sets for each book. The difference between this option and "processed" is that the labels and pockets would not come already affixed to the book.

Catalog Cards: Books processed with cards only means that a set (usually one shelflist card, one title card, however many subject cards the book is deemed to require, a joint author card and/or illustrator card if required, and two main entry cards) will be packed with each book shipped.

In schools with adequate library media programs the titles selected for the literature-based reading program would already be in the collection and thus in the card catalog or database. The new paperbacks ordered for the reading program would be entered into the existing inventory and designated accordingly so there is no need for catalog card sets on these duplicated titles. Cards, pockets, labels, lamination, and hinges are needed and can be done quickly and inexpensively at the building or district level.

PROCESSING

CHECKING OUT READING BOOKS

Whether paperbacks for the literature-based reading program are checked out of the library media center by a teacher or a student, the record of that borrowing is kept and the responsibility for the return of the books is that of the borrower. If the student is the borrower, the library will hold that student responsible for that uniquely numbered copy; if a teacher is the borrower, she or he is responsible for however many uniquely numbered copies were borrowed. In a computerized library circulation system there are designated unique numbers for both the borrowers and each individual piece of material in the collection. In non-computerized circulation systems the transaction card is inserted in the circulation file after borrowing occurs.

GREEN CARDS

In the case in which the teacher has borrowed a number of copies for students' use, how will the teacher know which of the copies borrowed and distributed to the students went to which student? Lists are time-consuming to make and difficult to use. A green card (or any other identifiable colored stock set aside for this purpose) which is already in the pocket of each book is signed by the student and held by the teacher for the period of use. With a computerized circulation system, green cards and pockets would be needed for the literature-based reading books; with a non-computerized system, two transaction cards per pocket would be needed for each book—one card for the circulation file and a green card for the teacher's benefit. If a student has left a book at home when reading class begins, an additional copy may be checked out *for just that period*. That copy is signed out at the charge desk by the student who is then responsible to the library media center for that copy as soon as the reading period ends.

Since many students will be reading duplicate copies of a title, they may pick up books which they believe to be theirs. But turning in *a* copy is not the same as turning in *the* copy which was given to you. A clear understanding of this on the part of the teachers and students will not solve the problem of an inadvertent mistake, but it will curtail theft, because students must pay for the uniquely numbered copy given to them (and for which they signed) if it is lost, stolen, or vandalized. Paperbacks purchased with public funds are public property; those which the students buy for their own use will not be laminated, labeled, dotted, or stamped, so there is no confusion.

DOTTING FOR IDENTIFICATION

Since dozens of paperbacks are returned to the library media center each day it is necessary to identify quickly those which belong to the literature-based reading program. Colored adhesive-backed dots are available from all library and/or office supplies vendors. In our school orange dots are used, and paperbacks thus marked are sorted at the charge desk and immediately shelved in the workroom with the others of their kind on the appropriate grade level shelves. It is there that the teachers often browse and plan which title(s) will be used next.

MENDING

As the books are being reshelved they are also examined to see if they need mending. Any that do are attended to immediately, and then the book is shelved. Should a student tear a page or break the spine of a book so that several pages or signatures come loose, that student should be sent to the library media center and the mending can be done on the spot. By attending to the mending as needed, the number of copies of a title on the shelf plus those being used in a classroom (listed in the circulation file or the computer) are all that the school owns, and there is no other place to look. By calling the library media center, at any time, a teacher may learn how many copies of a desired title are in and who has those that are charged out.

IN-HOUSE PROCESSING

Any paperback may be bound by a book bindery and almost all titles can be purchased prebound (from suppliers that specialize in prebound paperbacks). Either of these options adds a great deal to the cost, perhaps doubling it. This defeats the whole purpose of using paperbacks so that the lesser cost will allow for more titles. Either option also provides a sturdy cover with the same cheap paper pages of the original paperback. Often the binding is so tight the printing nearest the binding cannot be read, and the student will crack or break the binding to see the words. Another consideration is the added weight and bulk, since students carry paperbacks in their pockets, purses, and backpacks.

BOOK POCKETS

Book pockets for the transaction cards are available from library supply vendors with imprinted school name and address and adhesive backing for only slightly more than the cost of plain pockets. This self-sticking type eliminates the need for glue, paste, or water. The school's name plus address will ensure return if a book winds up at another library. It may not deter theft, but it will be highly identifiable as school property.

Pockets should be placed on the body of the book, never on the inside of the covers. The body of the book has the strength to withstand stamping and slipping, while the covers, with that same activity, tear away from the book. A century ago pockets were placed in the back of the book because they were considered ugly and defacing. Today we are concerned with service, efficiency, and speed. That means the pocket belongs in the front on that first page. With paperbacks that sometimes means you cover over the title page, credits, advice to parents, a blurb, etc. So be it. If that material is really vital or necessary, a photocopied image can be made and pasted in the back cover. Pockets in the front eliminate that tedious performance at the desk of turning them over and then turning them back.

STAMPING

A possession stamp bearing the name of the school in a single line is used to stamp the bottom, side, and top edges of the pages. This will identify the book as school property without even opening it. Note: it is important to take the book as it lies face-up and stamp bottom, side, top—in that order. This will ensure that the stamping reads correctly from all sides as it lies on a table, on a seat in the school bus, on a desk top, etc. If it is stamped top, side, bottom, the stamping will read upside-down. Of course, if the book is lying face-down the correct stamping will not read properly, but most of the time books are left face-up.

LAMINATING

A very satisfactory method of adding to the life and use of paperbacks is affixing the type of cold laminate which can be purchased from any large library supply vendor. This material is made of clear plastic with an adhesive backing, is very easy to use, and comes in rolls of various widths. Like other contact laminates, it is backed by a waxed paper which you remove after cutting to size. But the difference between this material and others you may have used to cover shelves, line drawers, decorate walls, etc. is that this special material does not "fix" immediately and can be moved and adjusted. After a few hours it adheres permanently or, if you are in a hurry, you can get instant adhesion with a tacking iron or even a child's toy iron which gets warm but not hot. Labels should be put on before the lamination which seals them away from picking fingers. The colored dots which identify these paperbacks as belonging to the literature-based reading program, however, should be put on top of the lamination and covered with clear tape. This will enable a title to be dropped from the list and those books integrated into the regular collection.

HINGING

Before the pockets are put into the paperbacks the hinging should be done. The hinges are made out of a length of 1-1/2 or 2-inch-wide clear plastic tape often referred to as Scotch Tape thereby giving an unsolicited ad to the 3M company. Many tape manufacturers make such a clear polyester tape. Mylar is more expensive and not needed for this use. Do *not* use a tape which is milky white and translucent. That tape is for mending pages and does not have the tensile strength for hinging.

Cut the tape (unless the tape dispenser has a very sharp serrated blade) slightly shorter than the height of the book and affix it to the inside of the cover and the first page of the book. Do the same with the inside of the back cover and the last page. Make sure the book is lying open flat each time. These hinges will help keep the covers on through many circulations.

LABELING

Labeling for the literature-based reading paperbacks should be the same as as that which is done for the library media center books. The support staff personnel are used to the process and, should the title be dropped from the literature-based reading program list at some future date, the books will be ready for the library media center collection once the identifying dot is removed. Call number, author, title, and individual identification number can all be typed easily, quickly, economically, and with a low incidence of error by using the self-sticking labels which are approximately 2-1/2-inches long by 1 inch high and come 33 to a page (three across and 11 down). These sheets are frequently used for envelope addresses printed by office machines or computers. Three identical labels are typed across the sheet which are used as follows: 1 for the transaction card; one for the book pocket; and one for the spine label which is applied *at the very bottom* of the spine.

It is important that the typing always begins at the left edge of the labels. There can be no misunderstanding about those directions. Then, when the label is placed on the bottom of the spine, the label curves around to the front of the book and even the thinnest paperback will still show several numbers/letters of the call number and author's name. The barcode will be placed inside the book, either above or below the card and pocket, where idle fingers may pick less frequently. The individual identification number for the labels is the barcode number.

Pica type (ten-pitch) is too large for labels. Most libraries use elite type (12-pitch) but 15-pitch type, which is one size smaller, is still better for it allows more words to the line while the lines carry the same spacing. Thus, the typeface is smaller but there is more *white space* and better legibility.

BIG BOOKS AND LITTLE BOOKS

The Big Books and Little Books used primarily in kindergarten and first grade are put together with three to four staples (much like weekly news magazines) and very quickly come apart. It is wise to apply additional staples at the start of the processing procedures so that there are at least five—some opening to the inside and some to the outside of the book. The largest staplers sold by library suppliers or office supply houses are still not long enough for the Big Books and some bending of the cover and pages is required. When the stapling is finished the same tape that is used for hinging should be placed over the staples down the full length of that inside page. This will help to keep the sheets from tearing loose from the hinges. A similar application of a wider width of the same tape is needed for the outside (spine) to cover the staples and help keep the cover intact.

The Little Books, which are for the children, should also be hinged and laminated as described above. Whether the Big Books need to be laminated could be debated, since the Big Books are most often handled by the teachers. But these Big Books are extremely expensive and fragile. If the lamination will protect the covers and lengthen their lifespan, it is well worth the time and trouble and will delay the inevitable mending.

THE ROLE OF PARENTS

As with any curriculum program, engaging the support and understanding of the parents in the school district is a critical element. This is not always as simple as it might sound. We have the disadvantage of being engaged in a service with which most parents have had some personal experience, namely school. They may either consider themselves experts to some extent about how it all should work or they may register resentment and suspicion because of their own negative school experiences. While this may appear to be a sour note upon which to start this section, it is a reality educators live with daily. As a result, parents and educators sometimes become polarized instead of joining forces to create the most effective program for the children.

The role of the school administrator in this case cannot be overlooked. In addition to creating an atmosphere in which teachers and curriculum specialists can work productively, this leader must also create an active and positive climate of trust, communication, and mutual reinforcement between home and school. This is quite a challenge, but met well, it can chart the way to a successful school program.

PRESENTATION TO PARENTS

The first step is to plan—with the Parent Teachers Association president—an evening presentation for parents on the how and the why of literature-based reading instruction. The purpose of the presentation is to win parents over to a new way of thinking about reading instruction, so the presenter should be carefully chosen. If the person who spoke to the teachers at the start is available and willing to speak to parents, that might be a good choice. If that is not a possibility and there is no faculty member or district language arts specialist who is capable and willing to do this, the same suggestion follows here as was given when addressing this issue with teachers. Check with the professional organizations of reading educators such as, The International Reading Association, the National Council of Teachers of English,and Teachers Applying

Whole Language (TAWL), all of whom have affiliates at both the state and local levels who can supply the names of presenters on this topic. Also, don't forget to contact the reading professionals in the school and/or district who also may have contacts in this area. The important point here is something that was emphasized earlier in talking about the professional development of faculty members: the presenter must be reassuring and credible to the audience and must be able to effectively convey the message and respond with calm good humor to doubts that will be expressed. If this introduction is not done well, it could set up barriers to the successful undertaking of the literature-based program. So select the presenter with great care.

THE TWO-PRONGED APPROACH

In a a two-pronged presentation, the topic of Process Writing should be addressed first. As was mentioned earlier, if a sound writing program is not in place, such as Donald Graves's Process Writing Approach, then much that has to be done in the literature program will come to a standstill. The coordination of writing with reading is essential to the success of the program. It seems best to implement the writing phase first, so it should be presented to the parents as a first course.

The second talk should address the literature-based reading program, with a number of points to be touched upon. First, the reason for moving in that direction—the *why* of the argument. There certainly is enough research to support this point and much of it has been presented in the first and second chapters of this book. Second, *how* it will be done should be clearly explained with enough detail to leave parents with an understanding about how it will differ from what is presently in place. However, since many parents do not know specifically how reading is taught, the treatment here, while it should not be as in-depth as that which is given for teachers, should clearly explain the difference between the old and the new approaches. For example, the presenter might indicate that as teachers move into greater use of trade books and less reliance on the basal system, worksheets will gradually be replaced by samples of their child's writing.

When asked the inevitable question about how they will know their child's reading level, it is best to reply that the reading tests currently in place in the district will continue to be used. While we know that these tests generally do not give us an accurate picture of the child's reading ability, until the whole issue of assessment is seriously discussed at the district and state levels, it is acceptable to use this response and leave it at that. While you want the presentation to inspire the parents to think in new ways about reading and language arts instruction, consideration must be given to their concerns that their child's education will not be jeopardized by an educational fad. Give them a picture of a well-thought-out program that has the child's needs and the establishment of lifelong literacy as the driving force behind the change. Assure them that the skills will be addressed and that each child's progress will be closely monitored. Its potential for greater and more effective parent/home involvement in a child's learning is one of the most attractive and important aspects of the literature-based reading program. Thus, the third topic that should be discussed is the parents' role in all of this. The following sections address this important topic.

PARENTS AND EARLY READERS

Becoming a Nation of Readers, the national report on the status of reading in the United States, made reference to the impact of a child's preschool experiences:

> Reading begins in the home. To a greater or lesser degree, depending upon the home, children acquire knowledge before coming to school that lays the foundation for reading. They acquire concepts for understanding things, events, thoughts, and feelings, and the oral language vocabulary for expressing these concepts. They acquire the basic grammar of oral language (Andersen, et al. 1985, 21).

A home environment rich in both the spoken and written word and reading enjoyment modeled by the parents has been cited by many researchers to be a prime factor in the development of lifelong readers.

Benjamin Bloom studied the growth of certain human characteristics in his longitudinal studies of 1,000 individuals who were measured or observed at different points in their development. He studied such characteristics as intelligence, height, weight or aggressiveness. He found that "for a number of the most significant human characteristics the most rapid period of growth appears to be in the first seven years of life" (Bloom 1981, 104). Bloom focused on the importance of the early preschool years for intellectual growth and reminded us that children entering first grade have already passed through the most rapid period of growth in their lives. Parents and families can still provide tremendous stimulus and support to the prereader and beginning reader. No child should be pushed into learning to read without plenty of preliminaries, and encouraging parents to provide these is a major joint task of daycare and other preschool teachers and, if the child is lucky, librarians. What kinds of preliminaries, then, are appropriate for the prereading child to build a base for learning reading skills?

THE PARENT'S ROLE

The importance of continuous spoken language with the young child cannot be overemphasized. Parents and/or adult caregivers are not just the first teachers in the child's life, they are also the role models and standard bearers. Many research projects have shown overwhelmingly the beneficial outcome of enriched speech practiced by adults with infants and toddlers resulting in larger vocabularies and understanding of concepts. When children enter school with this background they are ready to move on to the reading and writing aspects of their development. Beginning students who are not familiar with such familiar topics such as in/out, above/below, hot/cold, and others face a struggle to master both vocabulary and concepts before any other language instruction can be attempted. A veritable stream of speech should accompany all interactions of adults with infants. Scandinavian/American research with six-month-old infants has clearly demonstrated that even at that early age the babies are able to distinguish familiar speech patterns and pronunciation from those of another tongue.

When a mother takes her child out for a walk in a stroller and describes what they see in language rich with adjectives and adverbs, she is imparting knowledge of color, size, movement, and shape variations. For example: "See the blue van parked at the curb? A van is a small truck. The blue van belongs to a TV repair company. Perhaps they have come to fix a broken TV in that brown house." Contrast this with a situation in which the adult waits to be asked, "Whazzat?" and answers, "That's a truck." When the child is in the care of an adult other than a parent, instructions should be given regarding the need for conversing with the child. It is as important as a hat and mittens for winter outdoor outings. Some parents may hope that sitting the child in front of the television set will accomplish the same purpose but, alas, small children get sidetracked by the motion (especially in cartoons and commercials) and the *language* of the voice-over or the characters makes little impact and is depersonalized.

The value of reading aloud has been stated here and a thousand other places. That means *all kinds* of reading aloud. Dad may be willing to share a part of the evening paper by reading aloud the report of last night's football game or the comics. Setting aside time for reading for the whole family will allow parents to read uninterrupted while prereading children pretend to read their books. This is an excellent time for older siblings to read to the younger. Many schools set aside time for fifth and sixth graders to read to primary students. Teachers are enthusiastic about the benefits to both the readers and the listeners.

Don Holdaway, whose thoughts about whole language were quoted earlier, tells something of what it can mean to a preschool or older child to be read aloud to by a parent or other significant adult:

> From the child's point of view the situation is among the happiest and most secure in his experience, The stories themselves are enriching and deeply satisfying—there is something emancipating in the experience which transcends normal time and space. It provides the expansion of mental room, and freedom within it. The nature of the relationship with the parents is very special to the situation: the parent is giving complete attention; there are none of the normal distractions most of the time; the parent is invariably positive and interesting, with an enhanced being from association with the richness of the literature; and there is a feeling of security and special worth arising from the quality of the attention being received. *Thus the child develops strongly positive associations with the flow of story language and with the physical characteristics of the books* (Holdaway 1979, 39-40).

What Holdaway is pointing out is the importance of this early experience on the literacy development of children. Reading to children at home creates not only an understanding of books—how print moves from left to right, how dialogue differs from text description, how letters all have sounds in our language—but it also gives the children a sense of story, the concept of the sequence of story. They learn that there are characters who act and speak to accomplish certain ends, and the concept of a plot which defines a problem and reaches a resolution. The overall impact of this experience is the positive feeling that the children gain about books and the satisfactions of reading. The children begin to think of themselves as readers and begin to practice reading behavior, thus the tendency to want to read the same story again and again until it is memorized. This is a very positive by-product of this experience and it should be encouraged.

As their interest in books and print increases with daily exposure to reading with the parent, the children may become interested enough in print to start experimenting with letters on their own. Children then begin to write. What a wonderful natural transition. Holdaway comments on this part of the process:

> During the leisurely period of three to four years of active literacy-learning before school entry most of these children become fascinated in print as a mystery that is well worth solving. They begin to play with writing in the same way as they play with reading, producing writing-like scribbles, the central feature of which, for them, is that it carries a message. They learn to write their names, and explore creating letters and letter-like symbols with a variety of writing devices. They show intense interest in the print around them on signs, labels, advertisements, and TV, and often imitate these forms in inventive ways. By the time they enter school they are likely to know the alphabet and be able to recognize many of the letters in both lower and upper case forms, and name them (Holdaway 1979, 47).

So parents should be encouraged to provide their children with plenty of paper and writing implements, whether they be pens, pencils, crayons, or magic markers, to begin their journey into the world of making words on paper.

All of these by-products, that is children becoming aware of the significance of print and seeing themselves as readers and writers, come from the simple task of a parent sitting daily, if only for a brief period, and reading to the child. When the children identify themselves as readers and writers at an early age, they enter formal schooling inclined toward literacy, and receptive to learning more about this mysterious process that older brothers and sisters, parents, and other significant adults in their lives do. In every sense of the word they are ready to read and, in many respects, eager to become better readers. Holdaway refers to this receptivity as a *Literacy Set*. He defines a *set* "in this psychological sense to mean an ability to tune in with appropriate action (Holdaway 1979, 49). For teachers who work with these young children, the experience is filled with pleasure.

PRESCHOOL HABITS OF EARLY READERS

In 1958 Dolores Durkin began a study of early readers to find out what went on in their homes during the preschool years which had an impact on their early success as readers. She did a second phase of this study in 1961. The questions Durkin sought to answer were: What kinds of children tend to be early readers? From what kinds of families do early readers come? Her research, done in both California and New York, showed that intelligence quotient was not a factor in this process. She says of the IQ factor:

> It would be natural to assume that precociousness in reading is one manifestation of intellectual superiority. And indeed the median IQ's of the two groups of early readers in the research were high (121 in California and 133 in New York). However, within the groups, the IQ scores showed great variation. The significance of the wide ranges of IQ scores (91 to 161 in California and 82 to 170 in New York) must not be overlooked (Durkin 1966, 134).

As to the type of family that early readers come from Durkin found some similar characteristics surfaced among the families as the result of the family interview:

> . . .parents of early readers showed greater willingness to give early help. They also showed less tendency to believe that reading should be taught only by a trained person. A most important factor here, however, was their additional belief that a child's own interest in

becoming a reader lessens the need for special training on the part of a person who might help (Durkin 1966, 135).

Her research further revealed that children in these families had their questions about a variety of topics answered on a regular basis. She also noted that the role of older siblings in this process was very important and that a smaller age difference seemed to result in a greater likelihood of help being given. In response to the question about the socioeconomic level of the families of early readers, Durkin found that this was not clearly seen as a determining factor. In summary, she states:

> What is much more important, the research data indicated, is the presence of parents who spend time with their children; who read to them; who answer their questions and their requests for help; and who demonstrate in their own lives that reading is a rich source of relaxation, information, and contentment (Durkin 1966, 136).

Durkin's main findings are restated here for the sake of brevity. The early readers in this study:

1. Moved through a progression of phases from scribbling and drawing to copying objects and letters of the alphabet to asking frequent questions about spelling and finally gaining the ability to read.
2. Asked many questions about spelling and used ordinary size pencils and pens as well as small blackboards.
3. Expressed continued interest in letters and words, and their parents tended to talk more about sounds of letters which sometimes proved to be productive, but not always.
4. Seemed to go on interest binges, that is, they stayed with a particular phase of letter and word development for long periods of time until it no longer interested them.
5. Had their interest in words stimulated in many ways such as seeing them on TV, on billboards, food packages, menus, phonograph records, cars, and trucks.
6. There was a trend toward girls showing interest in topics having to do with the home or playing store and

the boys being curious about words having to do with what was typically considered *at that time* "male" subjects, such as cars and air and space travel.

RECOMMENDATIONS

In summary, it is important to note that the role of the parent in the child's preschool years is critical to their literacy development. Our recommendation in this regard for parents of young children is very much in keeping with the work of both Holdaway and Durkin. We suggest that parents consider the points raised by these two reading experts and take to heart the importance of reading to their child from an early age, answering their questions about letters, words and ideas, and providing them with writing utensils of all sorts so that they can experiment with writing letters and words. We strongly criticize the use of workbooks, flash cards, and reading programs designed to make their child a reader earlier. These will only serve to create a negative impression about reading which will ultimately result in ground being lost or never being gained at all.

PARENTS AND THE ELEMENTARY SCHOOL CHILD

As children move through the grades in elementary school, their attitudes toward reading will go through many phases. Again, the parent plays a vital role in sustaining interest and development. Sometimes parents assume that because their child is receiving formal reading instruction their responsibility to the child in this regard is lessened or even over. Quite the contrary is the case. Parent/family reinforcement during this period is essential as is continuing at home those practices which characterized the years before school. Bedtime story sessions should continue for many years after school begins. With this in mind, we cite here the essence of recommendations by the National Commission on Reading which presented its findings in the report *Becoming a Nation of Readers* on the topic of how parents can help their children become good readers:

1. Help children acquire a wide range of knowledge by taking them on trips to the zoo, museums and other cultural places.
2. Talk with your children about these and other experiences.
3. Encourage your children to think about events by describing them.
4. Read aloud to your children (well beyond the preschool years).
5. Provide your children with writing materials (including a quiet place in which to write).
6. Encourage watching TV shows that have educational value (and watch with them on a regular basis).
7. Monitor the amount of TV that your children watch and the types of programs watched.
8. Monitor your children's school performance through conferences with teacher(s).
9. Encourage your children to read independently and silently. Not all home reading should be oral. In fact, at least 15 to 20 minutes of silent reading a day should be expected if the children are to maintain the gains made during in-school instruction. If they are to become good at it, we should insist that they practice just as they would with a sport or learning to play an instrument.
10. Continue your personal involvement in your children's growth as readers.

The suggestions that are offered are applicable to children no matter what reading program is used in their school. If parents have an understanding of what a literature-based program is offering their child, there should not be a problem about how they can get more involved at home. Parents can readily be involved in the literature-based reading adventure at school also. The team of teacher and librarian arranges many reading activities in which parents can take part.

BOOK DISCUSSIONS

Discussing books with readers has become a popular aspect of reading programs with upper elementary and middle school students. Many teachers have called upon parents to assist with these programs and the parents have enjoyed the books as well as the interaction with the students. Some schools have held book discussion sessions with parents and other adults interested in learning about children's literature, especially books that have become standard favorites since their own youth. This has enabled the adults to make informed suggestions for what the youngsters might like to read and to share reactions to the books.

STORYTELLING

Storytelling is an artform that all children should be exposed to with regularity. For nursery school, kindergarten, and first grade children it is a marvelous way to stimulate listening skills. With no pictures to look at they must concentrate on the storyteller and create pictures in their own minds. Their grandparents did this with radio and had much more acute listening skill development than T.V. watchers whose images are all created for them. Books with illustrations on every page and ubiquitous television do not demand much imagination.

Schools that invite adults in to read or tell stories can showcase individuals who represent diverse cultures. They should be encouraged to bring artifacts and stories about their own childhoods to share with the children. Grandparents can sometimes be more effective than parents since the time when they were young seems so very long ago. For some reason World War II captures the fancy of little boys more than any other conflict. A few souvenirs and words from a real veteran are powerful drawing cards.

BOOKTALKS

Booktalking is a marvelous device for interesting potential readers: preschoolers, parents-to-be, beginning readers, elementary and secondary students, and adults of all ages. It is most effective when done on a one-to-one basis with an individual, of course, and has been done for decades by library media specialists as they show their wares to potential readers. This impromptu reading guidance is at its best when the professional knows the collection and the patron. It is a promotional experience that demands, in addition to the knowledge of the materials, all of the insights and skills of a good salesperson (how far to go, when to back off, matching interests, and so on). Parents want to know about children's books and are keenly interested in seeing not only the newest publications but also the Golden Oldies. Many of the latter will be ones they recall from their own childhood and they want to know whether children are still interested in those books and at what age. Both parents and grandparents seek guidance in what to buy for birthdays, Hanukkah, or Christmas gifts. They are particularly uninformed about reference materials for children and welcome any advice that a library media specialist can and will offer. Families really appreciate being given the opportunity to come to the library media center, after school if necessary, to examine reference books. If a trial drive is a desirable prerequisite to buying a car, why shouldn't parents and children handle reference books in order to make intelligent additions to the home library?

SCHOOL VISITS

Parents also enjoy attending storytelling sessions with their children. If the library media specialist holds regular weekly storytelling sessions for kindergartners and first graders the schedule will be made early in the fall, perhaps even before school opening. An announcement of that schedule should be sent to all those parents inviting them to join their children's classes, hear the story, and help the children in selecting materials. Parents enjoy the experience, gain a better understanding of the library media program, and provide the much needed extra personnel in dealing with the individual needs of the children.

A group of parents, eager to have their beginning readers choose award-winning books, met with their library media specialist who suggested that all the Caldecott Medal and Honor Books have bright red dots affixed to their spines. Thus, those parents who wanted to pick them off the shelves with ease could do so. Or, if they wanted to urge their children to bring home red-dotted books among their selections, the means were in place. Rather than have the staff affix the dots, the library media specialist provided both the dots and the complete lists of the books to each member of the group who had agreed to come in and dot the books. This method took longer to complete the task, but the few parents who participated learned a great deal about those books and also how many of them were in the library media center's collection. They also became aware of what a large percentage of those titles were in the literature based reading program.

MEETING TODAY'S CHALLENGES

Being a parent in today's world is probably the most challenging task known. Not only are there societal challenges facing children and young adults, there are also equally challenging demands facing parents. It is almost impossible to maintain a family today without two incomes. As a result, many parents cannot spend the quality at-home time with their children that their parents likely spent with them. This reality requires parents to make choices about how they address their children's needs. Most of what we are suggesting to parents is a part of good family communication. It demands little money but does demand some quality time. Most parents are willing to give the time if they feel it will produce results. We urge parents to consider the suggestions offered here, well grounded in solid knowledge and research on literacy development, and therefore having considerable merit and potential for success. Those of us who have worked with children for any number of years can verify that children who have the at-home experiences recommended here ultimately become better readers. They also, it is hoped, become lifelong readers and writers.

7 ANSWERS TO SOME LINGERING QUESTIONS

There are significant issues related to changing the reading instruction program from a basal approach to one that is literature based that must be handled firmly if the program is to succeed. Depending on how they are dealt with they can make or break a program. Some of these issues are:

- Assessment of students
- Censorship
- Integration of language arts with content
- Impact on the district's student testing
- Strategies to handle and prevent resistance to the program.

ASSESSMENT

If a basal reading system is being used in your school district, you are familiar with the end-of-unit, end-of-book tests. These tests are designed primarily to determine whether or not students have learned the skills presented in the lessons suggested in the teacher's manual and are given, as their titles suggest, at the end of the unit or book. For example, if the teacher taught the long "a" sound in that unit, there would be a subtest that would assess whether or not the student had learned to identify the long "a" sound. It might look something like this:

The children are asked to look at three pictures of objects which are named by words having a long "a" vowel sound. They are told to say the name of each picture to themselves and circle any picture which has a long vowel "a" sound. Generally speaking, the pictures have little relationship to the graphic representation of words let alone seeing those words in the context of larger connected text. As students move through the school year, the pictures would probably be replaced by groups of words which each child would be expected to sound out and match to a picture. The point is, then, that the test has little to do with the real-life skills of reading.

Winograd and Paris (1988) write about the strides we have made in reading instruction in the past 15 to 20 years and the lack of improvement in reading assessment that has occurred. They state the problem that has developed this way:

> The essence of the problem is that teachers are trying to obtain useful instructional information from tests that were originally designed for sorting individuals along some continuum from those who score highest to those who score lowest. . . . In short, tests designed to rank students select items that differentiate skilled from less-skilled readers but they provide little insight into a child's ability to understand, appreciate, or use text material for authentic purposes (Winograd & Paris 1988, 2).

To fully understand the impact of the research upon the assessment of reading we have to consider how instruction in reading has changed so radically. In the past, reading was considered an act which was influenced very little by the reader. Rather, it was thought that all that was necessary for comprehension to occur was the ability to decode the words, have a well developed ability to attach meaning to the word symbol, and be able to follow the sequence of the story or text. What the reader brought to the task or in what way interacted with the text, were not issues.

Today we see reading as an interactive process in which the reader brings to the text a host of experiences which influence prior knowledge of the topic being addressed. If we accept this fact, we must change the way we teach reading. In a more traditional model of instruction the teacher taught a skill, the child practiced the skill and the teacher tested the skill, all done in isolation. In the present model given to us by Pearson and Gallagher (1983) we see the student and teacher functioning in this way.

With this model of comprehension, the student assumes more responsibility for reading as the strategies presented by

---

> ## A Model of Explicit Instruction
>
> ### Proportion of Responsibility for Task Completion
>
> | *All Teacher* | *Joint Responsibility* | *All Student* |
> |---|---|---|
> | Modeling | Guided Practice | Practice or Application |

the teacher become second nature. The focus in this model is on ultimate independence for the reader. Teaching skills in isolation, therefore, must give way to teaching skills in context with instructional strategies. If we follow this line of thinking, then, we must also change the way in which we assess students. The Wisconsin Reading Association published a monograph on assessment in which they comment on this point:

> The interactive model of reading comprehension implies that reading instruction must guide the reader to use all available sources of information to read. Depending upon the purpose of reading which is influenced by the reading context, the reader should set comprehension goals, activate background knowledge, recognize the structure of the text, and activate strategies to aid comprehension. . . .If reading assessment is to reflect the interactive model of the reading process, it should consider the factors which influence comprehension:. . .prior knowledge. . .text structure. . .reading strategies. . .interests and attitudes. . . .Current research suggests that in order to interpret reading comprehension scores, the factors which affect comprehension should be measured concurrently (Wisconsin Reading Assoc. 1990, 4-8).

WHY ASSESS READING?

The first question we have to ask about reading assessment is: Why are we doing it? In fact, we are going to have a variety of responses to this question all of them valid. Those of us who work in public school districts know that there are three constituencies that have an interest in testing. First of all we have the board of education and the administration who are concerned with accountability. Then we have the parents who are also interested in accountability and in seeing how well their child stacks up against the rest of the world. Then, of course, we have the teachers who are interested in learning about the child and using this information to plan for further instruction. Each of these constituencies has legitimate concerns about testing. What usually happens is that, rather than addressing the concerns of each group, we set about jamming them against each other in a fight for dominance. It is rare that any group ever takes the time to legitimatize or to listen to the concerns of the others.

For the moment, however, let us think about the reasons for testing from an educational point of view. It is safe to say that the primary reason we test or assess students is to have some measure of how well they are learning. If we find out that they are not learning, then we must design some instruction that will remedy that situation. If we find out that they are learning, we then know that it is safe to take them further. Therefore, the first thing to find out is what we are measuring. Yetta Goodman says about evaluation:

> Whole Language teachers know that evaluation is going on all the time; it is built into the plans every day. It is integral to the process of teaching and learning not a separate, discrete activity (Goodman, et al. 1989, 6).

Up to this point, we have seen reading as a process of understanding printed matter, both fiction and nonfiction, using a number of skills which are considered integral to the process. These skills come under two main headings: vocabulary and comprehension. Under vocabulary would fall phonics skills, word recognition, and word meaning. Under comprehension would be found the skills of finding the main idea, drawing conclusions, making inferences, and determining the author's purpose. This is a simplified version of the process but it will serve our purposes here. All of these skills have been traditionally found on standardized reading tests in isolated subtests. As a result, they have been the focus of instruction for reading through the basal manuals which teachers have traditionally used for planning lessons. However, we refer back to the list of items offered by the Wisconsin text regarding the changes in reading instruction which have come about in the past 15 years as a result of the research.

In the interactive model of reading, there is a series of functions going on which are essential to the comprehension process. If these functions are overlooked, a great deal of information about the reader's ability as a reader is lost.

Indeed, if we ignore these items, we will fail the reader. These processes are not easily assessed but they must be seen as an essential part of the evaluation process. We refer here to the reader's ability to activate prior knowledge, the ability to determine the structure of a text while reading, the ability to use the metacognitive strategies to assist in problem solving while reading. Let us consider some ways to legitimately assess students' reading ability.

AUTHENTIC FORMS OF READING ASSESSMENT

The first point is the importance of using authentic text for assessment. This text should consist of pieces which are presented in their entirety, as opposed to excerpts, and they should communicate information that is real, not fabricated, for the purpose of the test. If we are encouraging the use of entire authentic text in reading instruction then we must also consider it essential to the assessment process.

What do we mean by authentic texts? Essentially we mean text that is as close as possible to reading that the student might do in a normal reading setting. It may be fiction or nonfiction and it should be written in normal, well-formed language. We are excluding here stilted, vocabulary-controlled pieces of text. In addition, the text should be structured in such as way that it will provide opportunities for the student to think at the inferential and evaluative levels of thought and not focus on the literal level as many standardized tests do.

When appropriate test materials have been chosen, the next step is to determine how to organize the testing situation to get the information desired. In traditional standardized test situations, the student is provided with a portion of a larger piece of text and is normally asked to choose an answer to a question from among a list of multiple choice responses. For example, a third grade child might be asked to read the following passage:

Mr. Jones felt sad when he went past the stores on High Street. They were different from his shop around the corner. They had large shiny new products. In his store there were only old things that no one wanted to have any more.

He often said to himself, "I wish I had new things in my store. When people came in they would want to buy what I have because they are new and shiny not old and dull."

Mr. Jones thought about how he could get some new things for his store that would make it seem brighter.

One day a little boy came into the shop and told him he was looking for a toy truck for the town he made for his railroad tracks. He said he wanted one that looked old because the town was old and it would look more like a real town that way. Mr. Jones showed him a a truck that had been brought to him the day before. The boy was very excited. He told Mr. Jones that this would make his railroad town perfect. When he left Mr. Jones felt better about his shop. "Not everybody is looking for shiny new things," he said.

Following the reading of the passage, the child would be asked the following questions and, among the choices in each set, to choose one answer.

Mr. Jones ran a:
1. Gas Station
2. Store for used things
3. Grocery Store
4. Dairy

What was Mr. Jones sad about?
1. His dog had died
2. He did not like to walk to work
3. The weather was bad
4. He did not have new things to sell in his store

The boy came into Mr. Jones store to find:
1. A truck
2. A ball
3. A baseball bat
4. A train

For those children who have learned how to take tests, there is every possibility that they might get the answer correct, not because they truly understand the passage, but because they probably made the right choice by the process of elimination. In itself that indicates a level of brightness which tells us that this child will probably succeed in spite of us. Then there is the child who simply makes a lucky guess and does well on the test but who is incapable of understanding the passage. Not only does this type of test give us incorrect information about the child, but it does not give the teacher or reading specialist any information about the child's ability or areas of weakness. This child might easily go unnoticed for several years and the reading problem could go untreated if it were not for the information garnered by the classroom teacher in other informal reading settings.

RECOGNIZING GOOD READING-ASSESSMENT INSTRUMENTS

Sheila Valencia, a national authority on reading assessment, gives us some criteria to consider when developing an assessment package. Sound assessment:

- Must be anchored in authenticity—authenticity of tasks, texts, and contexts;
- Must be a continuous, on-going process that chronicles development;
- Must be multidimensional—committed to sampling a wide range of cognitive processes, affective responses, and literacy activities;
- Must provide for active, collaborative reflection by both teacher and student (Valencia 1990, 338-339).

Chittenden (1990) gives us a schema of reading assessment which he breaks down into three major categories: observation, performance samples, and tests. Under *Observations* he places things that teachers see happening which relate to literacy development on a daily basis as they work with the children in the classroom. These can be things that the children say or do which reflect their understanding and their thinking. Under *Performance Samples* he lists things that give concrete evidence of their accomplishments such as what they write, make, draw, or construct. Finally, under *Tests* he places both formal tests which are commercially produced and informal assessments such as reading inventories, quizzes, or end-of-unit tests.

OBSERVATIONS

While it is not our intention to minimize the importance of observation, we will not spend a great deal of time exploring it simply because it is such a natural part of good teaching and most teachers do it naturally. What is important to keep in mind, however, is finding a way to keep track of what is observed. When it comes time to report on those precious observations at a parent conference or special services meeting for the child, the teacher will better serve the child if the report contains considerable documentation of the daily reading behavior of the child. In a day already overloaded with essentials, that is a hard thing to ask a teacher to do. Its importance cannot be overlooked, however. Chittendon suggests that there are several areas of the instructional day in a primary classroom that would yield information about a child's literacy development:

- Story-time: teacher reads to class (responses to story line; children's comments, questions, elaborations).
- Independent reading book-time (nature of books child chooses or brings in; process of selecting; quiet or social reading).
- Reading group/individual (oral reading strategies, discussion of text, responses to instruction, conferences).
- Writing (journal, stories, alphabet, dictation, invented spelling).
- Informal settings (use of language in play, jokes, storytelling, conversation).
- Books and print as resource (use of books for projects, attention to signs, labels, locating information) (Chittendon 1990, 28).

PERFORMANCE SAMPLES

Performance assessments, according to the state of Colorado, "demonstrate a student's ability to integrate and apply what has been learned" (Colorado State Department of Education 1990, 7). In the area of language arts, we translate that type of assessment to mean Portfolio Assessment, a subject that is receiving considerable attention nationally not only in reading but in other content areas as well. What are portfolios and how do they work? Again we turn to Sheila Valencia, to give us an idea of what they are. She tells us that portfolios are:

> . . .like a large expandable file folder that holds (a) samples of the student's work selected by the teacher or the student, (b) the teacher's observational notes, (c) the student's own periodic self-evaluations, and (d) progress notes contributed by the student and teacher collaboratively (Valencia 1990, 339).

The next question becomes: What kinds of samples of childrens work would go into it? Winograd and Paris give us some suggestions for this:

1. Lists of books, magazines, and other materials the child has read throughout the year.
2. Lists of topics and authors that the child enjoys.
3. Audiotapes and charts of the child's developing oral reading fluency.
4. Interviews and checklists designed to assess children's motivation and attitudes toward reading.
5. Assessments of children's abilities to apply reading strategies flexibly, appropriately, and independently.
6. Interviews that focus on the child's ability to engage in self-evaluation.
7. Compositions, speeches, debates, or discussions that extend information gleaned from reading.
8. Results of other formal and informal tests (Winograd and Paris 1988, 1-2).

In the state of Vermont during the 1990-91 school year portfolio assessment was introduced statewide. In the area of writing, teachers across the state were trained in assessing the products of students' written work. In addition to the writing portfolio, a best piece of writing is selected by each fourth and eighth grade student who then writes a letter about that piece of writing. In addition, each fourth and eighth grade student writes to a uniform prompt. In each portfolio will be placed three pieces of writing from the current school year in draft form but not necessarily revised form. The choice of tho pieces is to be made by the student with the assistance of the writing teacher. The teacher then will assess the students' work based on the pieces of writing submitted. The criteria used to assess the writing is based on four questions that the assessors must ask when looking at a student's portfolio:

1. Is the organization suitable to the writer's purpose?
2. Does the writing exhibit a sense of personal expression?
3. Does use of specific detail add to clarity?
4. Does the final draft exhibit an awareness of appropriate usage, mechanics and grammar? (Vermont Department of Education 1990, 9).

During subsequent school years there will be many aspects of the program to work out but the important things to remember about the project are that classroom teachers participated in designing it and it is an attempt to offer alternatives to standardized assessment. There is no question that judging these writing pieces will not be simple; in fact, that may prove to be a challenge far greater than anyone imagines. In an article describing the Vermont project, Mills tells us that "Scoring work portfolios is a matter of professional judgment. Judgment has to be calibrated against standards the profession shares and the public understands and supports" (Mills 1989, 10). In Connecticut, judging writing samples based on a holistic score has been in effect for several years and has proven quite a task for state mastery test scorers. This, however, is not our primary focus here so we will move on.

TESTS

The third type of assessment suggested by Chittendon is tests. The word alone is so rife with emotion for the population at large that it is virtually impossible to discuss this issue without distressing oratory. Part of the problem is probably due to the fact that so many of us had negative experiences with testing when we were in school. However, it is a fact of life in schools and one which must be part of the whole picture of the child. As mentioned earlier, how it is addressed will depend in great part on who is considering it. For teachers it has meaning on two levels. First, it is a part of the learning process and essential to gauging the student's growth. Second, (and this is sometimes overlooked) it is a measure of the teacher's performance or accountability. For parents and administrators, tests are also a measure of the children's growth and they judge a teacher's performance based on how well the class does on standardized tests. At a higher level, for members of the Board of Education and the tax-paying public, it is simply a measure of accountability. The Wisconsin Reading Association suggests that we look at accountability in this way:

> Accountability should be based on how much each individual grows over a given period of time, not on how many children are above average (a situation which may actually represent less growth). We should all (teachers, parents, students, administrators) be held accountable for maximizing the growth of students by providing them with the support, the expertise, and the respect they need and deserve to realize their full potential and take their place in an increasingly complex society (Wisconsin 1990, 42).

The point to be made here regarding testing is that there must be a willingness to focus in a major way on the instructional aspects of testing as well as the accountability component. If that point is recognized, then the importance of developing a testing program that reflects the instructional program will fall naturally into place.

EARLY LITERACY

The issue of using standardized tests with young children has received negative reviews of late. The Wisconsin State Reading Association suggests these reasons why these tests are inappropriate for young children:

1. Children are often confused by the directions.
2. The format of the standardized test is complex and unfamiliar.
3. The atmosphere for standardized testing is unsupportive.
4. Standardized tests fail to reflect the developing knowledge and skills of young children.
5. Observations of young children while they are taking standardized tests reveal that some accidentally score

high when randomly marking responses. (Wisconsin 1990, 33-34).

For those school districts using a literature-based reading system, the following recommendations are given for testing instruments to use in the early grades: in kindergarten the *Concepts About Print Test*, and in first and second grade the *Running Record* both of which have their origins in the whole language movement.

Concepts About Print Test (Kindergarten)

Originally designed by Marie Clay to be part of a larger survey of early reading behaviors, this test is used to look at only one aspect of the larger process of early literacy development. It checks the child's development of print awareness in relation to books. The skills addressed include:

- The ability to identify the front of a book;
- Awareness that print not pictures tells the entire story;
- Understanding what function letters and words serve;
- Understanding what is meant by the first letter in a word;
- Recognizing the difference between big and little words;
- Understanding the function of the space between words;
- Understanding the uses of punctuation such as the full stop (period), the question mark, and the "talking marks" (quotation marks).

In this test the child is presented with one of two small texts, one titled *Sand* and the other *Stones*. As the teacher reads the text, the child is asked certain questions about the text. For example, the child is given the book and asked to "show me the front of the book." Then the examiner tells the child that she will read the story and asks the child to tell her where the story begins. As they move through the story, the teacher will ask the child to do certain tasks such as "show me where to start" or "which way do I go?" On some of the pages there are intentional mistakes in the text or in the pictures which accompany the text. The child is asked to explain what is wrong with the text. The child is also asked what the various punctuation marks are for, and be asked to "find a little letter like this," or to "show me just one word" and then "now show me two words." There are 24 tasks in the test and it is given individually. After scoring, the child's performance is compared to that of children in the same age range. It is a developmentally oriented test and may be given whenever the teacher feels it is appropriate (Clay 1979).

Running Records (Grades 1 and 2)

Echoing the point made earlier, reading testing should imitate authentic reading situations as much as possible. The *Running Records* (Clay 1979) test does just that. When the record is given, the child is handed a text from the classroom collection which the teacher feels is appropriate to the pupil's level of development. It is understood that the child is in the early stages of reading development and therefore will be able to read the text. As the child reads the text out loud, the teacher is recording his or her progress using a set of prescribed marks. For example, a child reads from a book the following passage:

> Late at night the small animal
> crept along the ground and came
> to a spot in the bushes
> that had an opening
> near the pond.

As the child reads the story, the teacher is keeping track of correct readings and mistakes, or miscues as they are called. For each correctly called word a check is given. For incorrect words, whatever the child says is printed above the area where the miscue occurred. If the child self-corrects, that is noted on the record. Should the teacher give assistance with the word after several attempts by the child, that also is noted.

The information on what the child is doing while reading is far more valuable for the teacher than performance on a test where the child circles a picture that is named by a long "a" vowel sound. If a child is self-correcting during reading, that is important information. One who is using visual cues in the text is practicing strategies which are integral to the reading process. The important part is that the information being gleaned is given in a real reading situation, so it is safe to say that whatever the child is or is not doing is something that goes on whenever the child reads. For the most part the stress of a test situation will not be felt by the child because the test situation is no different from a normal reading experience. There would be stress of course if reading is difficult for the child, and that is not something that is picked up in a one-dimensional paper and pencil test. Indeed, in that situation if the child is consistently lucky and regularly picks the right answer, true ability to handle print could be hidden for years. With the *Running Record*, nothing can be hidden, it is all out there for the teacher's observation. The one component of the reading process that is not addressed by the *Running Record* is the child's ability to understand the message of the text. To adjust for that, many teachers ask questions after the child has read the text and note the reader's responses.

Those teachers who have used the *Running Record* format have found the marking system suggested by Marie Clay cumbersome. For one thing, it is difficult afterwards for anyone to know exactly what words the child missed and what other errors were made because the text used in the test is not available to the person reviewing the results. Another common complaint is that the symbols used are not personal enough to the teacher, in other words they don't have meaning. A suggestion for the first problem is to set aside certain texts from the classroom collection and type a copy of the first 100 to 150 words onto a sheet which will be used as the score sheet. As the child reads, the teacher makes the marks on the sheet just above the words. This sheet is then placed in the child's portfolio or reading folder and gives clear indication to all who read it where the student's strengths and weaknesses lie. Regarding the second issue of the symbols used, teachers can use their own symbols provided that they are posted for all to see and are commonly agreed upon by all who work together on the *Running Records*. The best thing to do is to have all teachers who give *Running Records* meet and discuss the symbols to be used by the entire group. What has to be kept in mind is that these records are read by a variety of people and need some consistency if they are to maintain their wide value.

PROCESS READING TESTS (GRADES 3 ON UP)

In reaction to the research on reading that has been done in the past 15 years, several states have instituted reading assessment models that mirror the goals stated for the reading programs in those states. In Illinois, Michigan, and more recently, Maryland and Connecticut, state level assessments are taking on a whole new complexion. Moving away from the standardized test multiple choice format, the new assessments have taken on a more global response pattern. In Illinois the tests are modeled on the interactive process of reading discussed earlier. The tests take into account not only the test itself but also the reader and the context in which the reading is done. For example, the reader element of the assessment includes the "attitudes about reading and the topic being read. . . the existing knowledge about the topic. . . the [reader's] ability to read the text. . ." and the reader's "knowledge of strategies to use to facilitate understanding" (Illinois 1988). The text element refers to the topic, the genre, the difficulty of the text and "the 'considerateness' of the text" in the sense of its organization and conciseness. The context of the assessment is a combination of the purpose for reading, how the comprehension of the text by the student will be demonstrated, and the physical surroundings in which the test is taken. Illinois has designed its reading assessment around these issues and presents this format for the test:

- Topic familiarity survey
- Passage to be read
- Constructing meaning (Comprehension) questions
- Reading strategies section
- Survey of reading and writing experiences (Illinois 1988, 5).

Michigan also has adopted the *Reader, Text, Context* model and has recommended to its school districts that an important part of the reading process is the opportunity to "elicit retelling that demonstrates knowledge of the key elements of the text" and "Nurture the logical responses instead of right or wrong answers" (Michigan 1987).

Maryland has designed its reading assessment in such a way that it is "interdependent upon other language processes—listening, speaking, and writing. The criterion-referenced assessment instrument to be used to assess reading should provide opportunities for discussion and written interactions with peers and teachers" (Maryland State Department of Education n.d.).

How does a performance reading test differ from a standardized reading test? In its simplest format it will begin with an *entire* piece of text rather than a portion of the text. Second, it will ask the reader to *respond in writing* to a set of questions which go beyond the level of initial understanding into developing interpretation, personal reflection and response, and on to demonstrating critical stance (Maryland n.d.). For example, if the student had read a fiction story, he or she might be asked to respond to questions such as these:

- What was this story about? Write a summary of the story and include details about _____.
- Why do you think the author had the main character act as he did in this situation? Explain your answer in detail.
- Compare the the main characters in the story and show how they are alike/different.
- Tell what probably happened to _____ in the story after the story ends based on the information given about them in the story. Support your answer with information from the story.

For a *narrative* piece the questions might be similar to these:

- Briefly tell what the article is telling us about.
- Based on what you read about (the printing press) tell how this information could affect the way newspapers are processed today.
- If you were going to give advice to someone about the use of (hunting knives) what would you stress most? Explain your reason.
- Compare the facts on (how to build a fire) presented in this article and those presented in the previous article. Based on the information presented, give your advice about the best way to proceed.

SCORING

The next step in the process is scoring. As mentioned earlier in the discussion about portfolios, the scoring of written responses takes considerable preparation and time. However, the information gleaned from the tests is considerably superior in its ability to tell us what the student can and cannot do regarding reading. First of all, students cannot fake a response when giving a written response. If they understood what they read they will show it in the way they respond.

The method used for scoring process reading samples is holistic in nature, that is, it is based on a scoring system ranging from 0 to 4. For example, the scorer reads the response and gives a score of 1, 2, 3, or 4 depending on the quality of the response. The student's response is compared against a set of previously set criteria related to the content of the text whether it is fiction or nonfiction. The scorer must use the criteria to gauge each response. In some cases a separate score can be given for content and another for the quality of the writing. This method gives a clearer picture of the student's strength and weakness regarding the ability to respond in writing to text. Some examples of criteria would be those listed below which are modeled by the criteria used in the Silver Burdett & Ginn Unit Process Test Manual (1989):

Content Score

- 0 *No response*: An unintelligible response.
- 1 *Poor*: Nothing that the student wrote in any way comes close to the content of the story or narrative response.
- 2 *Weak*: Some of the content is close to the response suggested but it is lacking in many respects and tends to look spotty and disconnected.
- 3 *Adequate*: The answer has many of the points mentioned in the preestablished criteria and shows good comprehension.
- 4 *Strong*: This response has all the information recommended for a strong response including points which embellish the answer. It is clearly above the average.

Writing Score

- 0 *No Response*: An unintelligible response.
- 1 *Poor*: Indicates severe problems with the organization or the answer and obvious flaws in grammar and punctuation.
- 2 *Weak*: Poorly organized and some grammar and punctuation problems but sentence structure is fairly good and coherent.

- 3 *Adequate*: Sentence structure is good, sequence of thought is well done, and grammar and punctuation are adequate.
- 4 *Strong*: Superior sentence structure, grammar and punctuation is very well done, and the answer has an interesting and informative flow to it that places it apart from the average.

It takes both training and practice with this scoring before teachers can feel comfortable with it. It is a good idea to have someone sit with each teacher and give impressions of suggested scores for each student after the teacher has scored one or two questions. This scoring is difficult to do and requires a great deal of decision making. Hence the need for teachers to have someone to reflect with as they are being initiated into its use. It is important to remember that within each rating on the scale of 0 to 4 there is a range. Therefore, there will be strong and weak twos, threes, and fours. All of this requires decision making. Equally important to keep in mind is that the use of pluses and minuses with this scoring method is unacceptable.

One of the problems associated with holistic scoring is keep the score bias free. This is a difficult task when the teacher who gives the test is also the one who corrects it. It is almost humanly impossible to keep the teacher's daily interaction with the child from influencing perception of how well a child will do. To compensate for this tendency, a couple of things can be tried. First, assign to each child a number before giving the test. Second, have each teacher on a grade level exchange papers, correct them, and then return them to the home room teacher. The teacher who has the papers should be unable to tell whose paper it is with this system.

If there are several questions to correct and there are more than two or three teachers in a grade level, assigning one question to each teacher to correct for the entire grade level is a time saver. Teachers should find it easier to stay with one question and gain momentum with it rather than changing gears once the first question is completed. The important thing to remember with this type of scoring is that a set of criteria must be set beforehand and mutually agreed to by all teachers correcting the tests.

The issue of testing and assessment as it relates to literature-based reading is a topic about which volumes could be and have been written. Our purpose here is to give a survey of the possibilities of testing procedures that can be used with this type of program. There are many points which haven't been mentioned because the topic is beyond the scope of this book. However, there are many references cited which may be referred to for a fuller view of the assessment/testing movement that is underway in reading.

CENSORSHIP

The issue of censorship is not new to education, but public schools that use trade books in their reading program will be especially vulnerable to its sting. The glorious freedom of widening choices in any area of life always brings risks.
The International Reading Association recommends the following:

> The International Reading Association urges state and local education agencies to uphold the principle of intellectual freedom and to resist any effort to censor reading textbook series, or any other type of instructional materials, that have been carefully, systematically, and professionally judged to be valuable resources for teachers and children. Failure to retain or adopt such materials because of sincerely held but limited or biased views will restrict the ability of our schools to meet the needs of our children (IRA 1991).

With those thoughts in mind, IRA recommended these points:

> The determination of normal procedures for text selection should include development of the following:
>
> 1. There should be policies for the selection of printed materials. These policies should be developed with input from community groups, including teachers, students, parents and civic leaders. Policies must be written and approved by appropriate governing bodies (board of directors, trustees, etc.).
> 2. There should be written guidelines for identifying and handling complaints.

3. There should be a system for openly communicating with civic, religious, educational and political bodies in the community.
4. There should be systematic methods for disseminating positive information about intellectual freedom through newspapers, radio and television (IRA 1985).

It is point two in this list upon which we would like to focus, that is the need to have a written policy for handling complaints. If this policy or procedure is not in place when a book is challenged, the consequences for the school district could be (and have been for school districts in the past) traumatic. We recommend that the procedures include the following points which are based on the Connecticut State Department of Education's guide to re-evaluation of challenged materials:

1. Do not remove the challenged material from use in the instructional program, even after it has been challenged.
2. Set up a Censorship Committee composed of the school librarian, a parent, a classroom teacher, a curriculum supervisor if there is one, and a reading specialist. This committee will not handle the complaint, but they will act as coordinators and resources during the proceedings.
3. A form should be developed by the Censorship Committee which will be filled out by the person making the complaint. (See Appendix B)
4. The complaint will be handed on to the superintendent who will then set up an ad hoc committee to review the complaint and turn over their recommendations. Once this work is done, the committee will be disbanded.
5. The superintendent will then communicate the committee's decision to the person making the complaint.
6. If the person making the complaint does not agree with the committee's recommendations, that person may petition the board of education which may hold a special hearing to review the ad hoc committee's decision.
7. Throughout the process, it is important that the superintendent be the *sole spokesperson* for the district. This point is important because outsiders will try to get other people within the district and board members to speak about the issue. This could lead to very incendiary rhetoric which will do little to move the process

along. In many cases the whole procedure could grind a halt.

8. Once a book has been reviewed, the same material should not be subject to further review unless the Board of Education agrees to it.

The importance of having a policy and procedure in place cannot be stressed too strongly. School districts have gone through months of agonizing public debate over challenged material which eventually deteriorated into political infighting. This has a paralyzing effect upon teachers who may become reluctant to use a book or several books if they fear that they contain material which might be challenged by under-informed parents or those with a large political axe to grind. In our efforts to spread the word about the use of a wide range of good literature in our schools, we are often undertaking an educational program for the community, as well as for the children themselves. The literature-based reading instruction program trains children to choose, as well as to master reading techniques. It has emerged as the most effective plan for setting young people on the path to lifelong literacy.

APPENDIX A:
AN INTERPRETATION OF THE LIBRARY BILL OF RIGHTS

ACCESS TO RESOURCES AND SERVICES IN THE SCHOOL LIBRARY MEDIA PROGRAM

The school library media program plays a unique role in promoting intellectual freedom. It serves as a point of voluntary access to information and ideas and as a learning laboratory for students as they acquire critical thinking and problem solving skills needed in a pluralistic society. Although the educational level and program of the school necessarily shape the resources and services of a school library media program, the principles of the Library Bill of Rights apply equally to all libraries, including school library media programs.

School library media professionals assume a leadership role in promoting the principles of intellectual freedom within the school by providing resources and services that create and sustain an atmosphere of free inquiry. School library media professionals work closely with teachers to integrate instructional activities in classroom units designed to equip students to locate evaluate and use a broad range of ideas effectively. Through resources, programming and educational processes, students and teachers experience the free and robust debate characteristic of a democratic society.

School library media professionals cooperate with other individuals in building collections of resources appropriate to the developmental and maturity levels of students. These collections provide resources which support the curriculum and are consistent with the philosophy, goals, and objectives of the school district. Resources in school library media collections represent diverse points of view and current as well as historical issues.

Members of the school community involved in the collection development process employ educational criteria to select resources unfettered by their personal political, social or religious views. Students and educators served by the school library media program have access to resources and services free of constraints resulting from personal, partisan, or doctrinal disapproval. School library media professionals resist efforts by individuals to define what is appropriate for all students or teachers to read, view, or hear.

The school board adopts policies that guarantee student access to a broad range of ideas. These include policies on collections development and procedures for the review of resources about which concerns have been raised. Such policies, developed by persons in the school community, and the community at large, provide for a timely and fair hearing and assure that procedures are applied equitably to all expressions of concern. School library media professionals implement district policies and procedures in the school.

Adopted June 26, 1986
Board of Directors
American Association of School Librarians

APPENDIX B: CENSORSHIP COMPLAINT FORM

CITIZEN'S REQUEST FOR RECONSIDERATION OF A BOOK

Author: _____ Hardcover _____ Paperback _____

Title: _____

Publisher (if known): _____

Request initiated by: _____

Telephone: _____ Address: _____

City: _____ State: _____ Zip: _____

Complainant represents: _____ Self _____ Organization (name: _____

1.   To what in the book do you object? (Please be specific. Cite pages.) _____

_____

2.   What do you feel might be the result of reading this book? _____

_____

3.   For what age group would you recommend this book? _____

_____

4.   Is there anything good about this book? _____

_____

5.   Did you read the entire book? If not, what parts did you read? _____

_____

6.   Are you aware of the judgment of this book by literary critics? _____

_____

7.   What do you believe is the theme of this book? _____

_____

8.   What would you like the library to do about this book? _____

_____

9.   In its place, what book of equal literary quality would you recommend that would convey the same picture and perspective of our civilization?

_____

Signature of Complainant   Date of Complaint

_____   _____

This matter will be considered by the Library Board of Directors and the Librarian.   **139**

APPENDIX C: SUGGESTED TITLES FOR A LITERATURE-BASED READING PROGRAM

The following lengthy list is meant to assist teachers and librarians who would like to peruse some of the titles that have been used succesfully in order to determine what best fits their own needs. At the first grade level fiction and nonfiction titles have been separated, but at the second through sixth grade levels they are combined. Each grade level has a full range of offerings to meet interest and ability levels. This list is compiled from what has been or is being used at these grade levels. All titles are in paperback.

BIG BOOKS

AUTHOR	TITLE	PUBLISHER, DATE
Bridwell, Norman	Clifford's Family	Scholastic, 1984
Brown, Margaret Wise	Where Have You Been	Scholastic, 1984
Chase, Edith Newlin	New Baby Calf	Scholastic, 1984
Cowley, Joy	Grandpa, Grandpa	Shortland, 1980
Cowley, Joy	The Hungry Giant	Shortland, 1980
Cowley, Joy	The Jigaree	Shortland, 1983
Cowley, Joy	Meanies	Shortland, 1983
Cowley, Joy	Monster's Party	Shortland, 1983
Cowley, Joy	Mrs. Wishy Washy	Shortland, 1980
Cowley, Joy	One Cold, Wet Night	Shortland, 1980
Drew, David	Animal Clues	Rigby, 1987
Drew, David	Caterpillar Diary	Rigby, 1987
Drew, David	Creature Feature	Rigby, 1988
Drew, David	Hidden Animals	Rigby, 1988
Drew, David	Mystery Monsters	Rigby, 1987
Gelman, Rita Golden	Why Can't I Fly	Scholastic, 1985
Hoberman, Mary Ann	A House Is A House For Me	Scholastic, 1986
Hucklesby, Hope	It Came To Tea	Price Milburn, 1985
Hutchins, Pat	The Doorbell Rang	Scholastic, 1987
Hutchins, Pat	Rosie's Walk	Scholastic, 1987
Kalan, Robert	Jump, Frog, Jump	Scholastic, 1981
Mathews, Louise	Bunches of Bunnies	Scholastic, 1978
Melser, June	In A Dark Wood	Shortland, 1980
Melser, June	Lazy Mary	Wright Group, 1990
Melser, June	Sing A Song	Shortland, 1980
Melser, June	To Market, To Market	Wright Group, 1980
Parkes, Brenda	Who's In The Shed	Rigby, 1986
Parkes, Brenda / Judith Smith	The Enormous Watermelon	Rigby, 1986
Parkes, Brenda / Judith Smith	Jack & the Beanstalk	Rigby, 1986
Randell, Beverley	Ten Big Dinosaurs	Scholastic, 1985
Sendak, Maurice	Chicken Soup With Rice	Scholastic, 1962
Slobodkina, Esphyr	Caps For Sale	Scholastic, 1968
Wells, Rosemary	Noisy Nora	Scholastic, 1973

GRADE 1 (Fiction)

AUTHOR	TITLE	PUBLISHER,DATE
Averill, Esther	The Fire Cat	Harper, 1960
Bridwell, Norman	Clifford and the Grouchy Neighbors	Scholastic, 1985
Bridwell, Norman	Clifford Goes to Hollywood	Scholastic, 1980
Bridwell, Norman	Clifford The Big Red Dog	Scholastic, 1963

Bridwell, Norman	Clifford The Small Red Puppy	Scholastic, 1971
Bridwell, Norman	Clifford's ABC	Scholastic, 1983
Bridwell, Norman	Clifford's Halloween	Scholastic, 1966
Bridwell, Norman	Clifford's Riddles	Scholastic, 1974
Brown, Marc	Arthur's April Fool	Atlantic/Little, 1983
Byars, Betsy	Go and Hush The Baby	Viking, 1971
Carle, Eric	The Very Hungry Caterpillar	World Publishing
Cohen, Miriam	"Bee My Valentine"	Morrow, 1978; D/Y,1983
Cohen, Miriam	First Grade Takes a Test Series	Greenwillow, 1983; Dell, 1983
Cohen, Miriam	Liar, Liar, Pants On Fire	Greenwillow, 1985
Cohen, Miriam	Lost in the Museum	Greenwillow, 1979
Cohen, Miriam	The New Teacher	Macmillan, 1972
Cole, J.	The Missing Tooth	Random, 1988
Cowley, Joy	The Bicycle	Wright Group, 1983, 1990
Cowley, Joy	Clever Mr. Brown	Wright Group, 1981, 1990
Cowley, Joy	Copycat	Wright Group, 1981, 1990
Cowley, Joy	Danger	Wright Group, 1982, 1990
Cowley, Joy	Flying	Wright Group, 1981, 1990
Cowley, Joy	Go, Go, Go	Wright Group, 1983, 1990
Cowley, Joy	Grandpa, Grandpa	Wright Group, 1990
Cowley, Joy	Grizzly and the Bumble Bee	Wright Group, n.d.
Cowley, Joy	Grumpy Elephant	Wright Group, 1982, 1990
Cowley, Joy	The Haunted House	Wright Group, 1982, 1990
Cowley, Joy	Houses	Wright Group, 1983, 1990
Cowley, Joy	Hungry Monster	Wright Group, 1981, 1990
Cowley, Joy	I Want Ice Cream	Wright Group, 1981, 1990
Cowley, Joy	The Kick-a-Lot Shoes	Wright Group, 1981, 1990
Cowley, Joy	Mouse	Wright Group, 1983, 1990
Cowley, Joy	Nighttime	Wright Group, 1983, 1990
Cowley, Joy	No, No	Wright Group, 1982, 1990
Cowley, Joy	On A Chair	Wright Group, 1983, 1990
Cowley, Joy	Painting	Wright Group, 1983, 1990
Cowley, Joy	The Seed	Wright Group, 1987
Cowley, Joy	Sloppy Tiger and the Party	Wright Group, n.d.
Cowley, Joy	Stop!	Wright Group, 1982, 1990
Cowley, Joy	The Storm	Wright Group, 1983, 1990
Cowley, Joy	The Sunflower That Went FLOP	Wright Group, 1982, 1990
Cowley, Joy	The Tree House	Wright Group, 1983, 1990
Cowley, Joy	What's For Lunch?	Wright Group, 1983, 1990
DePaola, Thomas	Nana Upstairs and Nana Downstairs	Putnam, 1973
Eastman, Patricia	Sometimes Things Change	Childrens, 1983
Freeman, Don	Corduroy	Viking, 1968
Gag, Wanda	Millions of Cats	Coward-McCann, 1928
Gelman, Rita Golden	More Spaghetti, I Say!	Scholastic, 1977
Giff, Patricia R.	All About Stacy	Dell, 1988
Hamsa, Bobbie	Fast Draw Freddie	Childrens, 1984
Harrison, David L.	Wake Up, Sun!	Random, 1986

Hautzig, Deborah	Happy Birthday, Little Witch	Random, 1985
Hoff, Syd	Who Will Be My Friends	Harper, 1960
Johnson, Crockett	Harold's Trip to the Sky	Harper & Row, 1957
Johnson, Crockett	A Picture for Harold's Room	Harper, 1960
Lerner, Sharon	Follow the Monsters	Lerner, 1985
Lobel, Arnold	Days With Frog and Toad	Harper, 1979
Lobel, Arnold	Frog and Toad All Year	Harper, 1976
Lobel, Arnold	Frog and Toad Are Friends	Harper, 1970
Lobel, Arnold	Frog and Toad Together	Harper, 1972
Lobel, Arnold	Mouse Soup	Harper & Row, 1977
Lobel, Arnold	Mouse Tales	Harper, 1972
Lobel, Arnold	Owl At Home	Harper, 1975
Mahey, Margaret	My Wonderful Aunt Story 1	Wright Group, 1986
Mahey, Margaret	My Wonderful Aunt Story 2	Wright Group, 1986
Mahey, Margaret	My Wonderful Aunt Story 3	Wright Group, 1987
Melser, June	Fizz and Splutter	Wright Group, 1982, 1990
Melser, June	The Ghost and the Sausage	Wright Group, 1982, 1990
Melser, June	Help Me	Wright Group, 1980, 1990
Melser, June	Little Big	Wright Group, 1981, 1990
Melser, June	One, One, Is The Sun	Wright Group, 1983, 1990
Melser, June	Plop	Wright Group, 1981, 1990
Melser, June	Too Big For Me	Wright Group, 1982, 1990
Minariak, Else	Father Bear Comes Home	Harper, 1959
Minariak, Else	A Kiss For Little Bear	Harper, 1968
Minariak, Else	Little Bear	Harper, 1961
Minariak, Else	Little Bear's Visit	Harper, 1961
O'Connor, Jane	Lu, Lu And The Witch Baby	Harper & Row, 1989, 1986
O'Connor, Jane	The Teeny Tiny Woman	Random, 1986
Paris, Peggy	Dinosaur Time	Harper & Row, 1974
Petrie, Catherine	Hot Rod Harry	Childrens, 1982
Petrie, Catherine	Sandbox Betty	Childrens, 1982
Phillips, Jean	Lucky Bear	Random, 1986
Phillips, Jean	Tiger is a Scared Cat	Random, 1986
Rey, Margret	Curious George and the Dump Truck	Houghton, 1984
Rey, Margret	Curious George at the Fire Station	HM, 1985
Rey, Margret	Curious George at the Laundromat	HM, 1987
Rey, Margret	Curious George and the Pizza	HM, 1985
Rey, Margret	Curious George Plays Baseball	HM, 1986
Rey, Margret	Curious George Visits the Zoo	HM, 1985
Rey, Margret	Curious George Walks the Pets	HM, 1986
Ross, Pat	M & M and the Bad News Babies	Puffin/Penguin 1985
Ross, Pat	M & M and the Big Bag	Puffin/Penguin, 1985
Sendak, Maurice	Chicken Soup with Rice	Harper & Row, 1962
Seuss, Dr.	I Can Lick 30 Tigers Today	Random, 1969
Snow, Pegeen	Eat Your Peas, Louise!	Childrens, 1985
Thaler, Mike	A Hippopotamus Ate the Teacher	Avon, 1981
Vickers, Kath	The Wizard and the Rainbow	Wright Group, 1987

Viorst, Judith	Alexander and the Terrible, Horrible, No Good, Very Bad Day	Atheneum, 1972
Viorst, Judith	My Mama Says There Aren't Any Zombies, Vampires, Creatures, Demons, Monsters, Fiends, Goblins, or Things	Atheneum, 1973
Wiseman, B.	Morris Goes To School	Harper & Row, 1970
Ziefert, Harriet	Sleepy Dog	Random, 1984
Ziefert, Harriet	So Sick	Random, 1985

GRADE 1 (Nonfiction)

AUTHOR	TITLE	PUBLISHER, DATE
Althea	Birds	Longman, 1988
Althea	Fish	Longman, 1988
Althea	Flowers	Longman, 1988
Althea	Foxes	Longman, 1988
Althea	Lady Bugs	Longman, 1988
Althea	Snails	Longman, 1988
Althea	Swans	Longman, 1988
Althea	Trees	Longman, 1988
Cutting, Brian	Are You A Ladybug?	Wright Group, 1988
Cutting, Brian	Clouds	Wright Group, 1988
Cutting, Brian	The Dandelion	Wright Group, 1988
Cutting, Brian	Dinosaurs	Wright Group, 1988
Cutting, Brian	The Hermit Crab	Wright Group, 1988
Cutting, Brian	A Small World	Wright Group, 1988
Cutting, Brian	What Am I?	Wright Group, 1988
Cutting, Brian	Whose Eggs Are These?	Wright Group, 1988
Matthias, Catherine	Too many Balloons	Childrens, 1982
McLenighan, Valjean	Stop-Go, Fast-Slow	Childrens, 1982
Nash, Pamela	The Bird	Modern Curriculum Press, 1983
Nash, Pamela	The Bulb	Modern Curriculum Press, 1983
Nash, Pamela	The Butterfly	Modern Curriculum Press, 1983
Nash, Pamela	The Frog	Modern Curriculum Press, 1983
Nash, Pamela	The Orange	Modern Curriculum Press, 1983
Nash, Pamela	The Pony	Modern Curriculum Press, 1983
Nash, Pamela	Rice	Modern Curriculum Press, 1983
Nash, Pamela	The Seed	Modern Curriculum Press, 1983
Nash, Pamela	The Snail	Modern Curriculum Press, 1983
Nash, Pamela	The Spider	Modern Curriculum Press, 1983
Nash, Pamela	The Tomato	Modern Curriculum Press, 1983
Nash, Pamela	The Tree	Modern Curriculum Press, 1983
See How It's Made Series	The Bar of Chocolate	Modern Curriculum Press, 1983
See How It's Made Series	The Book	Modern Curriculum Press, 1983
See How It's Made Series	The Car	Modern Curriculum Press, 1983

| See How It's Made Series | The Cup and Saucer | Modern Curriculum Press, 1983 |
| See How It's Made Series | The Dress | Modern Curriculum Press, 1983 |

GRADE 2

AUTHOR	TITLE	PUBLISHER, DATE
Aardema, Verna	Bringing the Rain to Kapiti Plain	Dial, 1983
Aardema, Verna	Why Mosquitoes Buzz in People's Ears	Dial, 1975
Adler, David A.	Cam Jansen and the Mystery of the Dinosaur Bones	Dell, 1981
Adler, David A.	Cam Jansen and the Mystery of the Television Dog	Viking/Yearling/Dell, 1981
Althea	Desert Homes	Cambridge U. Press, 1983
Althea	Island Homes	Cambridge U. Press, 1983
Althea	Mountain Homes	Cambridge U. Press, 1983
Althea	Undersea Homes	Cambridge U. Press, 1983
Bemelmans, Ludwig	Madeline	Viking, 1960
Blume, Judy	The One in the Middle is the Green Kangaroo	Bradbury, 1981
Blume, Judy	The Pain and the Great One	Bradbury, 1984
Brown, Marcia	Stone Soup	Scribner, 1947
Clark, Ann Nolan	In the Land of Small Dragon	Viking, 1979
DeRegniers,	May I Bring a Friend	Atheneum, 1964
Erickson, Russell E.	A Toad for Tuesday	Lothrop, Lee, & Shephard, 1974
Gaeddert, LouAnn	Gustav the Gourmet Giant	Dial, 1976
Galdone, Paul	The Monkey and The Crocodile	Seabury, 1969
Hoban, Russell	A Bargain for Frances	Harper & Row, 1970
Hoban, Russell	Bedtime for Frances	Harper, 1960
Hoban, Russell	Bread and Jam for Frances	Harper, 1964
Keats, Ezra Jack	Hi, Cat!	Macmillan, 1970
Keats, Ezra Jack	The Snowy Day	Viking, 1962
Keats, Ezra Jack	Whistle for Willie	Viking, 1962
Kellogg, Steven	Pinkerton, Behave!	Dial, 1979
Kellogg, Steven	A Rose for Pinkerton	Dial, 1981
Kellogg, Steven	Tallyho, Pinkerton	Dial, 1982
Kent, Jack	The Caterpillar and the Pollywog	Simon, 1982
Lingren, Patricia	Pippi Longstocking	Viking, 1950
Lionni, Leo	Alexander and the Wind-up Mouse	Pantheon, 1968
Lionni, Leo	The Biggest House in the World	Pantheon, 1968
Lionni, Leo	Fish Is Fish	Knopf, 1970
Lionni, Leo	Frederick	Pantheon, 1967
Lionni, Leo	Swimmy	Knopf, 1963
Marshall, Edward	Fox All Week	Dial, 1984
Martin, Bill Jr.	Knots on a Counting Rope	Holy, 1990
McCloskey, Robert	Blueberries For Sal	Viking, 1948
McCloskey, Robert	Lentil	Viking, 1940

McCloskey, Robert	One Morning in Maine	Viking, 1952, 1962
McDermott, Gerald	Arrow to the Sun	Viking, 1974
McDermott, Gerald	The Stonecutter	Viking, 1975
Mosel, Arlene	The Funny Little Woman	Dutton, 1972
Mosel, Arlene	Tikki Tikki Tembo	Scholastic, 1968
Ness, Evaline	Sam, Bangs & Moonshine	Holt, 1966
O'Neill, Mary	Hailstones and Halibut Bones	Doubleday, 1961
Parish, Peggy	Amelia Bedelia	Harper & Row, 1963
Prelutsky, Jack	The Terrible Tiger	Macmillan, 1970
Preston, Edna Mitchell	Squawk to the Moon, Little Goose	Viking, 1974
Rylant, Cynthia	When I Was Young in the Mountain	Dutton, 1982
Sawyer, Ruth	Journey Cake Ho	Jr. Literacy Guild & Viking, 1953
Sharmat, Marjorie Wein	Nate the Great	Coward, McCann & Geoghegan, 1972
Sharmat, Marjorie Wein	Nate the Great and the Phony Clue	Coward, 1977
Smith, Robert Kimmel	Chocolate Fever	Coward, McCann, 1972
Steig, William	The Amazing Bone	Farrar, 1976
Steig, William	Amos & Boris	Farrar, 1971
Steig, William	Brave Irene	Farrar, 1986
Steig, William	Doctor DeSoto	Farrar, 1982
Steig, William	Roland the Minstrel Pig	Windmill Books., 1968
Steig, William	Solomon the Rusty Nail	Farrar, 1985
Steig, William	Sylvester and the Magic Pebble	Simon & Schuster, 1969
Stolz, Mary	Belling the Tiger	Harper, 1961
Ungerer, Tomi	Moon Man	Harper & Row, 1967
Waber, Bernard	Lyle, Lyle, Crocodile	Houghton, 1965
White, E. B.	Charlotte's Web	Harper, 1952
Williams, Barbara	Albert's Toothache	Dutton, 1974
Williams, Margery	The Velveteen Rabbit	Running Press, 1981
Williams, Vera B.	A Chair for My Mother	Greenwillow, 1982

GRADE 3

AUTHOR	TITLE	PUBLISHER, DATE
Adler, David A.	Cam Jansen and the Mystery of the Babe Ruth Baseball	Dell, 1982
Althea	Rain Forest Homes	Cambridge U. Press, 1985
Atwater, Richard Tuppe	Mr. Pooper's Penguins	Little, 1938
Balis, Andrea	P. J.	Dell, 1984
Blume, Judy	Freckle Juice	Four Winds, 1971
Blume, Judy	Iggy's House	Bradbury, 1970
Blume, Judy	Superfudge	Dutton, 1980
Bulla, Clyde Robert	The Chalkbox Kid	Random, 1987
Cleary, Beverly	Ramona and her Father	Dell, 1975
Cleary, Beverly	Ramona Quimby Age 8	Dell, 1982
Cleary, Beverly	Socks	Morrow, 1973

Cohen, Barbara	Molly's Pilgrim	Lothrop, 1983
Cooney, Barbara	Miss Rumphius	Puffin, 1985
Dahl, Roald	Charlie and the Chocolate Factory	Knopf, 1964
Davidson, Margaret	Helen Keller	Scholastic, 1969
Davidson, Margaret	Helen Keller's Teacher	Scholastic, 1965
Davidson, Margaret	Louis Braille	Scholastic, 1971
Estes, Eleanor	The Hundred Dresses	Harcourt, Brace & World, 1944
Fritz, Jean	And Then What Happened, Paul Revere?	Coward-McCann, 1973
Fritz, Jean	George Washington's Breakfast	Coward-McCann, 1969
Graeber, Charlotte	Mustard	Macmillan, 1962; Bantam, 1983
Greenwald, Sheila	The Meriah Delaney Lending Library Disaster	Houghton, 1977
Hoban, Russell	Dinner at Alberta's	Crowell, 1975
Hooks, William H.	Pioneer Cat	Random, 1988
Howe, Deborah	Bunnicula	Atheneum, 1979
Larrick, Nancy	Piping Down the Valleys Wild	Dell, 1968
Maestro, Betsy & Julio	The Story of the Statue of Liberty	Morrow, 1986
McClenathan, Louise	My Mother Sends Her Wisdom	Morrow, 1979
McCloskey, Robert	Burt Dow, Deep-Water Man	Viking, 1963
McCloskey, Robert	Time of Wonder	Viking, 1957
Monjo, F.	Secret of the Sachem's Tree	Coward, McCann & Geoghegan 1972
Parish, Peggy	Ghost of Cougar Island	Dell, 1986
Parish, Peggy	Haunted House	Dell, 1971
Parish, Peggy	Key to the Treasure	Dell, 1966
Robinson, Nancy K.	Wendy and the Bullies	Scholastic, 1983
Rockwell, Thomas	How to Eat Fried Worms	Watts, 1973
Ross, Pat	M & M and the Mummy Mess	Viking Penguin/Puffin, 1973
Sharmat, Marjorie	Maggie Marmelstein for President	Harper, 1975
Smith, Robert Kimmel	Jelly-Belly	Dell/Yearling, 1981
Thomas, Jane	The Comeback Dog	Bantam, 1981
Whelan, Gloria	Silver	Random, 1988
Yashima, Taro	Crow Boy	Viking, 1955

GRADE 4

AUTHOR	TITLE	PUBLISHER, DATE
Aiken, Joan	The Wolves of Willoughby Chase	Doubleday, 1963
Arkin, Alan	The Lemming Condition	Harper, 1976
Banks, Lynne Reid	The Indian in the Cupboard	Doubleday, 1980
Banks, Lynne Reid	The Return of the Indian	Avon, 1986
Bond, Michael	Paddington Helps Out	Dell, 1981
Cleary, Beverly	Dear Mr. Henshaw	Morrow, 1983
Clymer, Eleanor	The Horse in the Attic	Macmillan, 1954; Dell, 1985
Corbett, Scott	Lemonade Trick	Little, 1960
Dahl, Roald	The B F G	Puffin, 1982

Dalgliesh, Alice	Courage of Sarah Noble	Macmillan, 1954
Davidson, Margaret	Frederick Douglass Fights for Freedom	Scholastic, 1968
DeJong, Meindert	Wheel on the School	Harper, 1954
Eager, Edward	Half Magic	Harcourt Brace, 1954; Voyager, 1985
Estes, Eleanor	Ginger Pye	Harcourt, 1951
Fitzhugh, Louise	Harriet the Spy	Harper & Row, 1964
Garfield, James	Follow My Leader	Viking, 1957
Hamilton, Virginia	Zeely	Macmillan, 1967
Hurwitz, Johanna	Aldo Applesauce	Morrow, 1979
Hurwitz, Johanna	Baseball Fever	Morrow, 1981
Hurwitz, Johanna	Hurricane Elaine	Morrow, 1986
Langston, Jane	The Diamond in the Window	Harper, 1962
Lasky, Kathryn	Night Journey	Warne, 1981
Lawson, Robert	Ben and Me	Dell, 1985
Lawson, Robert	Rabbit Hill	Puffin, 1984
Lord, Athena V.	Today's Special: Z.A.P. and Zoe	Macmillan, 1984
Lord, Bette Bao	In the Year of the Boar and Jackie Robinson	Harper & Row, 1984
MacLachlan, Patricia	Arthur, for the Very First Time	Harper, 1980
MacLachlan, Patricia	Sarah, Plain and Tall	Harper & Row, 1985
Mathis, Sharon Bell	The Hundred Penny Box	Viking, 1975
Mowat, Farley	Owls in the Family	Little, 1961
Naidoo, Beverly	Journey to Jo'burg	Harper Trophy, 1986
Neville, Emily	It's Like This, Cat	Harper, 1963
Paterson, Katherine	Bridge to Terabithia	Crowell, 1977
Robertson, Keith	Henry Reed's Baby-Sitting Service	Dell, 1966
Wojciechowska, Maia	Shadow of a Bull	Macmillan, 19486
Pierce, Phillip	Bubble and Squeak	Scholastic, 1978
Sachs, Marilyn	The Bears House	Avon, 1989, 1971
Slote, Alfred	Rabbit Ears	Lippincott, 1982; Harper Trophy, 1983
Smith, Doris Buchanan	A Taste of Blackberries	Crowell, 1973
Speare, Elizabeth Geor	The Sign of the Beaver	Houghton, 1983
Sterling, Dorothy	Freedom Train	Doubleday, 1954

GRADE 5

AUTHOR	TITLE	PUBLISHER, DATE
Aiken, Joan	Nightbirds on Nantucket	Dell, 1966
Armstrong, William H.	Sounder	Harper & Row, 1969
Burch, Robert	Ida Early Comes over the Mountain	Puffin, 1980
Butterworth, Oliver	The Enormous Egg	Dell, 1956
Byers, Betsy	The Cartoonist	Puffin, 1978
Byers, Betsy	The Midnight Fox	Puffin, 1968
Byars, Betsy	The Summer of the Swans	Penguin, 1970

Collier, James Lincoln	My Brother Sam is Dead	Four Winds, 1974
Cooper, Susan	Greenwich	Macmillan, 1974
Forbes, Esther	Johnny Tremain	Houghton, 1943
Fox, Paula	The Slave Dancer	Bradbury, 1973
Frumgold, Joseph	Onion John	Crowell, 1959
Gardiner, John	Stone Fox	Crowell, 1980, Harper Trophy, 1983
Greene, Bette	Summer of My German Soldier	Dial Press, 1973
Hamilton, Virginia	The House of Dias Bear	Macmillan, 1968
Henry, Margaret	King of the Wind	Rand McNally, 1948
Hunt, Irene	Across Five Aprils	Berkeley, 1964
Kendall, Carol	Gammage Cup	Harcourt, 1959
Konigsburg, Elaine	From the Mixed-Up Files of Mrs. Basil E. Frankweiler	Atheneum, 1967
L'Engle, Madeleine	Many Waters	Farrar, 1962
L'Engle, Madeleine	A Swiftly Tilting Planet	Dell, 1978
L'Engle, Madeleine	A Wind in the Door	Farrar, 1973
L'Engle, Madeleine	A Wrinkle in Time	Farrar, 1962
Latham, Jean	Carry on, Mr. Bowditch	Houghton, 1983
Lewis, C. S.	Last Battle	Macmillan, 1956
Lewis, C. S.	The Lion, The Witch and The Wardrobe	Macmillan, 1965
Lewis, C. S.	The Magician's Nephew	Macmillan, 1955
Lewis, C. S.	The Horse and His Boy	Macmillan, 1965
Lewis, C. S.	Prince Caspian	Macmillan, 1951
Lewis, C. S.	The Silver Chair	Macmillan, 1965
Lewis, C. S.	The Voyage of the Dawn Treader	Macmillan, 1965
McCloskey, Robert	Homer Price	Puffin, 1976
O'Brien, Robert C.	Mrs. Frisby and the Rats of NIMH	Atheneum, 1971
O'Dell, Scott	Island of the Blue Dolphins	Houghton, 1960
O'Dell, Scott	Sarah Bishop	Houghton Mifflin, 1980
Parish, Peggy	Clues in the Woods	Macmillan, 1968
Parish, Peggy	Hermit Dan	Dell, 1977
Paulsen, Gary	Hatchet	Bradbury, 1987
Paterson, Katherine	The Great Gilly Hopkins	Harper, 1978
Reiss, Johanna	Upstairs Room	Crowell, 1972
Snyder, Zilpha Keatley	The Egypt Game	Atheneum, 1968
Snyder, Zilpha Keatley	The Headless Cupid	Dell, 1971
Snyder, Zilpha Keatley	The Witches of Worm	Atheneum, 1972
Speare, Elizabeth	The Witch of Blackbird Pond	Houghton, 1958
Taylor, Theodore	The Cay	Doubleday, 1969
Twain, Mark	Adventures of Tom Sawyer	Grosset & Dunlap, 1922

GRADE 6

AUTHOR	TITLE	PUBLISHER, DATE
Adams, Richard George	Watership Down	Macmillan, 1972

Aiken, Joan	Midnight is a Place	Viking, 1974
Alexander, Lloyd	The Book of Three	Holt, 1964
Alexander, Lloyd	Taran Wanderer	Holt, Rinehart & Winston, 1967
Babbitt, Natalie	Tuck Everlasting	Farrar, 1975
Bellairs, John	The House with a Clock in its Walls	Dial, 1973
Byars, Betsy	Pinballs	Harper & Row, 1977
Carroll, Lewis	Alice's Adventures in Wonderland & Through the Looking Glass	Grosset, Dunlap, 1984
Christopher, John	The City of Gold and Silver	Macmillan, 1967
Christopher, John	The White Mountains	Macmillan, 1967
Cooper, Susan	The Dark is Rising	Atheneum, 1973
Cooper, Susan	The Grey King	Atheneum, 1975
Cooper, Susan	Over Sea, Under Stone	Harcourt, 1966
Cooper, Susan	Silver on the Tree	Atheneum, 1977
Dahl, Roald	Danny: The Champion of the World	Knopf, 1975
Dickens, Charles	A Christmas Carol	Holiday House, 1983
Fleischman, Sid	The Whipping Boy	Greenwillow, 1986
Fritz, Jean	Homesick; My Own Story	Putnam, 1982
George, Jean Craighead	Julie of the Wolves	Harper, 1972
George, Jean Craighead	My Side of the Mountain	Dutton, 1959
Goodall, Jane	My Life with the Chimpanzees	Simon, 1985
Gray, Elizabeth Janet	Adam of the Road	Viking, 1942
Jenkins, Peter	Walk Across America	Morrow, 1979
Juster, Norton	The Phantom Tollbooth	Random House, 1961
Kelly, Eric Philbrook	Trumpeter of Krakow	Macmillan, 1928
London, Jack	Call of the Wild	Macmillan, 1960
Merrill, Jean	The Pushcart War	Dell, 1964
O'Dell, Scott	Sing Down The Moon	Houghton, 1970
O'Dell, Scott	Zia	Dell, 1976
Orwell, George	Animal Farm	Harcourt, 1946
Paterson, Katherine	Come Sing, Jimmy Jo.	Lodestar, 1985
Paterson, Katherine	The Master Puppeteer	Harper, 1975
Peck, Robert	A Day No Pigs Would Die	Dell, 1972
Raskin, Ellen	The Westing Game	Dutton, 1978
Rawls, Wilson	Where the Red Fern Grows	Doubleday, 1961
Saint Exupery, Antoine	Little Prince	Reynal, 1943
Selden, George	The Cricket in Times Square	Farrar, Straus, 1960
Snyder, Zilpha	A Fabulous Creature	Dell, 1981
Sperry, Armstrong	Call It Courage	Macmillan, 1940
Steinbeck, John	The Pearl	Viking, 1947; Bantam, 1956
Taylor, Mildred	Roll of Thunder, Hear My Cry	Dial, 1976
Twain, Mark	Prince and the Pauper	World Pub., 1948
Ullman, James	Banner in the Sky	Harper, 1954
White, E.	The Trumpet of the Swan	Harper, 1970
Yep, Laurence	Child of the Owl	Harper, 1976
Yep, Laurence	Dragonwings	Harper, 1974

REFERENCES

Adams, Marilyn Jager. *Beginning to Read*. Cambridge, Mass.: M.I.T. Press, 1990.

Anderson, Richard C., Elfrieda H. Hiebert, Judith A. Scott, and Ian A. G. Wilkinson. *Becoming a Nation of Readers: The Report of the Commission on Reading*. Illinois: The Center for the Study of Reading, 1984.

Assessment Reading in Illinois. Illinois State Board of Education, 1988.

Bartine, David. *Early English Reading Theory: Origins of Current Debates*. University of South Carolina Press, 1989.

Beck, I., M.G. McKeown, E.S. McCaslin, and A.M. Burkes. "Instructional Dimensions That May Affect Comprehension: Examples From Two Commercial Reading Programs." (Technical Report) Pittsburgh: University of Pittsburgh, Language, Reasearch and Development Center, 1979.

Bloom, Benjamin. *All Our Children Learning*. New York: McGraw Hill Book Co., 1981.

Byrne, Brian, and Ruth Fielding-Barnsley. "Evaluation of a Program to Teach Phonemic Awareness to Young Children," *Journal of Educational Psychology* 83, no. 4 (1991): 451-455.

Cambourne, Brian. *The Whole Story. Natural Learning and the Acquisition of Literacy in the Classroom*. Auckland, New Zealand: Ashton Scholastic, 1988.

Chall, Jeanne. *Learning to Read: The Great Debate*. New York: McGraw Hill, 1967.

Chittendon, Edward. "Authentic Assessment, Evaluation and Documentation of Student Performance," Association for Supervision and Curriculum Development Symposium on Assessment, California, April 4-5, 1990.

Clay, Marie M. *The Early Detection of Reading Difficulties*. Portsmouth, N. H.: Heinemann Pub. Co., 1979.

Cullinan, Bernice E., ed. *Children's Literature in the Reading Program*. Newark, Del.: The International Reading Association, 1987.

Downing, John, and Renate Valtin, eds. *Language Awareness and Learning to Read*. Springer Series in Language and Communication 17. New York: Springer-Verlag, 1984.

Durkin, Dolores. *Children Who Read Early*. New York: Columbia University, Teachers College Press, 1966.

———. "Ten Ways to Help Your Children Become Better Readers," University of Illinois: Center for the Study of Reading, n.d.

————. "What Classroom Observations Reveal About Reading Comprehension Instruction," *Reading Research Quarterly* 14, no. 4 (1978): 481-533.

Ehri, Linnea, and Claudia Rubbins. "Beginners Need Some Decoding Skills to Read Words by Analogy," *Reading Research Quarterly* 27, no. 1 (1992): 13-26.

Eldredge, J. Lloyd, and Dennie Butterfield. "Alternatives to Traditional Reading Instruction," *Reading Teacher*, Oct. 1986: 32-37.

Fielding, L., Paul Wilson, and Richard C. Anderson. "A New Focus on Free Reading: The Role of Trade Books in Reading Instruction," in *The Contexts of School Based Literacy*, edited by Taffy Raphael, New York: Random House, 1986.

Flesch, Rudolph. *Why Johnny Can't Read*. New York: Harper & Row, 1954.

Flood, James, ed. *Understanding Reading Comprehension: Cognition, Language, and the Structure of Prose*. International Reading Association, 1984.

Foorman, Barbara, David J. Francis, Diane M. Norvy and Dov Liberman. "How Letter-Sound Instruction Mediates Progress in First Grade Reading and Spelling," *Journal of Educational Psychology* 83, no. 4 (1991): 456-469.

Goodman, Kenneth S. *Language and Literacy: The Selected Writings of Kenneth S. Goodman*. Vol. I., New York: Routledge and Kegan Paul Ltd., 1982.

————. "A Study of Cues and Miscues in Reading," *Elementary English* 42, no. 6 (Oct./Nov. 1965): 639-643.

Goodman, Kenneth S., Yetta M. Goodman, and Wendy Hood. *The Whole Language Evaluation Book*. Portsmouth, N.H.: Heinemann Pub. Co., 1987.

————. *The Maryland School Performance Program*. Maryland State Department of Education. n.d.

Graves, Donald H. *Writing: Teachers and Children at Work*. Portsmouth, N.H.: Heinemann Educational Books, Inc., 1983.

Halliday, M.A.K. *Spoken and Written Language*. London: Oxford University Press, 1985, 1989.

Holdaway, Don. *The Foundations of Literacy*. Sydney, Australia; Aukland, New Zealand: Ashton Scholastic, 1979.

————. *Independence in Reading*. New York: Ashton Scholastic, 1980.

————. *Stability and Change in Literacy Learning*. Portsmouth, N.H.: Heinemann Educational Books, 1984.

Johnson, Edna, Evelyn R. Sickels, and Frances Clarks Sayers. *Anthology of Children's Literature*. Boston: Houghton Mifflin, 1970.

Johnson, Terry D., and Daphne R. Louis. *Litercy Through Literature*. Portsmouth, N.H.: Heinemann Pub. Co., 1987.

————. Institute for Teaching and Learning: Program Improvement Institutes—Language Arts Workshop. Connecticut State Department of Education, December 2-4, 1987.

Judy, Stephen N. *The ABCs of Literacy*. New York: Oxford University Press, 1980.

Kieras, David E., and Marcel A. Just. *New Methods in Reading Comprehension Research*. Hillsdale, N.J.: Lawrence Erlbaum Associates, Publishers, 1984.

Lesgold, Alan M., and Charles A. Perfetti, eds. *Interactive Processes in Reading*. Lawrence Erlbaum Associates, Publishers, 1981.

Macon, James M., Diane Bewell, and Mary Ellen Vogt. *Responses to Literature*. Newark, Del.: The International Reading Association, 1989.

Mills, Richard P. "Portfolios Capture a Rich Array of Student Performance," *The School Administrator*, December 1989: 8-11.

Newman, Judith. *Whole Language*. Portsmouth, N.H.: Heinemann Pub. Co., 1985.

Nicholson, Tom. "Do Children Read Words Better in Contexts or in Lists? A Classic Study Revisited," *Journal of Educational Psychology* 83, no. 4 (1991): 444-450.

Pearson, P. David, and M.C. Gallagher. "The Instruction of Reading Comprehension," *Contemporary Educational Psychology* 8 (1983): 317-344.

————. *Performance-Based Assessment Resource Guide*. Colorado Department of Education, Denver, Colorado, 80203, April, 1990.

————. *Reading at a Glance for Michigan Administrators*. Grand Rapids: Michigan Reading Association Curriculum Revision Committee, Michigan State Board of Education, 1987.

————. *Toward an Ecological Assessment of Reading Progress*. Wisconsin: Wisconsin State Reading Association, 1990.

————. *Unit Process Tests Manual: World of Reading Program*. Morristown, N.J.: Silver Burdett & Ginn. 1989.

Routman, Regie. *Transitions: From Literature to Literacy*. Melbourne, Australia: Rigby Pub., 1988.

Shannon, Patrick. *The Struggle to Continue: Progressive Reading Instruction in the United States*. Portsmouth, N.H.: Heinemann Pub. Co., 1990.

Smith, Nila Banton. *American Reading Instruction*. Newark, Del.: International Reading Association, 1986.

Tunnel, Michael O., "The Natural Act of Reading: An Affective Approach," *The Advocate* 5 (Winter/Spring 1986): 156-164.

Tunnel, Michael O., and James S. Jacobs. "Using Real Books: Research Findings on Literature-Based Reading Instruction," *Reading Teacher* 42, no. 7 (March 1989): 470-477.

Valencia, Sheila, "A Portfolio Approach to Classroom Reading Assessment: The Whys, Whats, and Hows," *Reading Teacher* 43, no. 4 (1990): 338-340.

———. *Vermont's Assessment Program*. W. Ross Brewer, Director, Vermont Department of Education, Montpelier, Vermont 05602, September, 1990.

Vellutino, Frank R. "Introduction to Three Studies on Reading Acquisition: Convergent Findings on Theoretical Foundations of Code-Oriented Versus Whole-Language Approaches to Reading Instruction," *Journal of Educational Psychology* 83, no. 4 (1991): 437-443.

Watson, Dorothy, and Constance Weaver. *Basals: Report on the Reading Commission Study*. New York: Richard C. Owen, Pub., Inc., 1988.

Werner, Patrice Holden, and Jo Anna Strother, "Early Readers, Important Emotional Considerations," *The Reading Teacher* 40, no. 6 (Feb. 1987): 538-543.

Winograd, Peter, and Scott G. Paris. "Improving Reading Assessment." *The Heath Transcripts*. D.C. Heath & Co., 1988.

Wray, David, ed. *Emerging Partnerships: Current Research in Language and Literacy*. BERA Dialogues: 4. Multilingual Matters Ltd., 1990.

INDEX

Bernice L. Yesner is the Library Media Director of the Beecher Road School, Woodbridge, Connecticut, winner of the 1991 School Library Media Program of the Year Award given by Encyclopaedia Britannica and the American Association of School Librarians.

Dr. M. Mary Murray is the Reading Consultant for the Newtown Public Schools and teaches graduate courses in Reading and Language Arts Curriculum and Instruction at Southern Connecticut State University.

Cover design: Apicella Design
Typography: Auerbach Typesetting